THE STRUCTURE AND MEANING OF SECOND BARUCH

SOCIETY
OF BIBLICAL
LITERATURE

DISSERTATION SERIES

Charles H. Talbert, Editor

Number 78
THE STRUCTURE AND MEANING
OF SECOND BARUCH

by
Frederick James Murphy

Frederick James Murphy

THE STRUCTURE AND MEANING OF SECOND BARUCH

Scholars Press
Atlanta, Georgia

THE STRUCTURE AND MEANING
OF SECOND BARUCH

Frederick James Murphy

Ph.D., 1984
Harvard University

Advisor:
John Strugnell

Library of Congress Cataloging-in-Publication Data

Murphy, Frederick James.
  The structure and meaning of Second Baruch.

  (Dissertation series / Society of Biblical
Literature ; no. 78)
  Thesis (Ph.D.)—Harvard University, 1984.
  Bibliography: p.
  1. Bible. O.T. Apocrypha. Baruch, 2nd—Criticism,
interpretation, etc. I. Title. II. Series: Dissertation
series (Society of Biblical Literature) ; no. 78.
BS1830.B4M87   1985   229'913   85-19589
ISBN 0-89130-844-X
ISBN 0-89130-845-8 (pbk.)

Printed in the United States of America
on acid-free paper

To my wife,
Leslie,
without whose help and support
this effort would have been far more difficult.

And to my parents,
Hazel and Jim,
whose continued encouragement
has sustained me
through the years.

Contents

Acknowledgments

Professor John Strugnell, my thesis advisor, has helped me tremendously by the sharpness of his insights, the breadth of his knowledge, and the generosity of his nature. Professor George MacRae's suggestions enabled me to explore areas I would otherwise have missed, and contributed to the clarity of my thought and expression. In the later stages of preparation, Professor F. M. Cross kindly read the manuscript and offered crucial observations, thus allowing me to avoid some major pitfalls.

To all three of these fine scholars I am deeply grateful.

1
Review of the Literature and Prospectus of the Thesis

INTRODUCTION

A full sixth-century Syriac manuscript of Second Baruch (including the epistle, chapters 78-87) was discovered by Ceriani in the last century and published by him in 1871.[1] The epistle itself is extant in several Syriac manuscripts.[2] In 1907, Kmosko re-edited the text, again including the epistle.[3] In 1973, Dedering produced another edition of Second Baruch, excluding the epistle. This last was used in this thesis. Passages from the epistle are taken from Kmosko's edition.

The Syriac text of Second Baruch claims to be a translation from the Greek.[4] Bogaert claims that the Greek was the language in which Second Baruch was originally written.[5] Charles and others posit a Semitic original behind the Greek.[6] In any case, since ours is a translation text, our ability to form arguments on the basis of language is limited. In this area we must proceed with great caution.

The English translation used in this thesis is that of Charles, with minor stylistic adjustments.[7]

---

[1] A. M. Ceriani, *Monumenta Sacra et Profana. Opera Collegii Doctorum Bibliothecae Ambrosianae*, tom. V, fasc. I/II, 1868/71.

[2] See R. H. Charles, *The Apocrypha and Pseudepigrapha of the Old Testament*, Volume II, Oxford: Clarendon, 1913, pp. 471-472. See also P. Bogaert, *Apocalypse de Baruch*, SC 144, 145, Volume I, pp. 43ff.

[3] M. Kmosko, ed., *Liber Apocalypseos Baruch filii Neriae . . . , Epistola Baruch filii Neriae*, Patrologia Syriaca 1:2, Paris: Firmin-Didot et Socii, 1907.

[4] See the words following the title in Syriac.

[5] Bogaert, Volume I, pp. 353-380.

[6] Charles, *APOT*, pp. 472-474.

[7] Charles, *APOT*, pp. 481-526.

In an attempt to avoid confusion, I shall consistently refer to chapters of Second Baruch using Arabic numerals. The numbers of chapters of the thesis will be written out, and modified by phrases such as "of this thesis." Sections of Second Baruch will be indicated by Roman numerals.

I accept the general consensus that Second Baruch was written in response to the destruction of the Second Temple.[8] It claims to be written in Palestine. I find no reason to deny this, although there is no compelling evidence concerning location. We do not know who the author was.[9] Obviously, he cannot have been Jeremiah's secretary Baruch, and so the work must be classed as a pseudepigraphon.

For the sake of convenience, I will abbreviate Second Baruch and Fourth Ezra as 2B and 4E respectively. Other abbreviations conform for the most part to those listed in the "Instructions for Contributors" of the Journal of Biblical Literature in JBL 95 (1976), pp. 331-346.

REVIEW OF THE LITERATURE

R. H. Charles

In 1896, R. H. Charles translated 2B into English, and provided the English text with an introduction and notes.[10] In 1913 he incorporated this, with some changes, into the second volume of his collection of the Apocrypha and Pseudepigrapha of the Old Testament. Charles' notes, with their helpful references to other works with similar ideas, are an invaluable starting point for any study of 2B. His broad acquaintance with a wide range of literature makes many of his remarks especially worthy of attention.

Following the earlier studies of Kabisch and de Faye, Charles splits 2B up into many different "sources."[11] By "source" Charles means an individual document. He finds at least six such documents brought together by the final editor in a scissors-and-paste manner to form 2B. His criterion for delineating the sources is a thematic one. In particular, the attitude of a given passage toward the future of Israel on earth characterizes that passage. The sources designated by him "A1," "A2," "A3," and "B1" are

---

[8]For a full discussion of the date of 2B, see Bogaert, Volume I, pp. 270-295.

[9]See the interesting suggestions of Bogaert, Volume I, pp. 438-444.

[10]R. H. Charles, *The Apocalypse of Baruch,* London: Black, 1896.

[11]Charles, *APOT,* pp. 474ff.

optimistic about Israel's future on earth, and sources "B2" and "B3" are pessimistic about it. The "A" sources look for a Messiah, whereas "B3" looks for a happy future, but in the world of incorruption. All sources designated "A" assume that Zion is still standing, and so are presumably written before the destruction of Jerusalem, but all sources named "B" assume that Jerusalem has already been destroyed, and so were written after 70 C.E.[12] The more detailed differences between the sources we need not explore here.

The problem with such a methodology is clearly stated by Sayler.[13]

> Charles' conclusions about the composite structure of 2 Baruch must be understood in the context of the multiple source methodology which was popular at the turn of the twentieth century. The basic axiom of this methodology was that a document must be internally consistent; the presence of differing viewpoints in any given work was attributed to the use of multiple sources by the author or redactor. . . . Subsequent developments in biblical research require that we modify Charles' conclusions about the structure of 2 Baruch. We now know that Jewish authors of the Greco Roman period frequently integrated a variety of sources and traditions into an individual document, with no attempt to harmonize different or even conflicting viewpoints. The use of several of these sources and traditions by any given author does not negate the literary unity of his work.

It must also be noted that although Charles posits so many sources, he never systematically interprets the work of the final editor. He frequently states that this editor has broken up the source documents and spliced them together in a new pattern, but we never get a redaction-critical picture of who this editor was and what were his Tendenzen, motives, and personal viewpoints. In spite of this, Charles tries to give a connected view of the "theology" of the book.[14] This effort is doomed to failure at the start because his method does not allow for a cogent interpretation of the book as a whole.

---

[12] *APOT*, p. 475.

[13] G. Sayler, *Have the Promises Failed?* SBLDS 72, 1984, pp. 3-7. At the time of the preparation of this manuscript for publication, I had only the "front matter" of Sayler's thesis in its published form available to me. Therefore, page references to her work are to the section in which the relevant material is found.

[14] *APOT*, pp. 477ff.

B. Violet[15]

In 1924, Violet did for 4E and 2B in German what Charles had done in 1913 in English for a wider group of texts. He translated the texts into German, and provided notes to the text as well as a short introduction for each work. However, Violet's notes are more specifically textual. In his introduction to 2B, Violet insists that the interpretation of 2B proceed from the assumption that it is a unified work.[16] Unfortunately, his introduction to 2B is not detailed or thorough enough to supply us with a convincing interpretation of it. Violet is preoccupied with the relation between 2B and 4E, but carries out his comparison in a fashion which borders on psychologizing, speaking, for example, on Ezra's need to be "calmed down" and of Baruch's "coldness."

A second important contribution of Violet to Baruch studies is his shifting of the ground of the concern about sources.[17] Rather than looking for complete documents within 2B, as did Charles, Violet looks for larger works from which 2B may have culled some of his ideas. He decides that Pseudo-Philo and 4E are the only documents which can qualify as sources for 2B.[18] He also suggests that we may be able to find smaller units within 2B which represent traditional material used by the author, and which are thus some of his sources. As examples he lists the visions of the waters and that of the cedar, as well as the descriptions of the endtime woes and blessings. He nonetheless concludes that at the time of his writing the scholarly world did not understand 2B well enough on its own terms to make convincing judgments about the limits of its source material.[19] His shifting of the way in which the source question was asked, thus rejecting Charles' atomism, paved the way for future studies of 2B.

A. Kolenkow[20]

In 1971 Anitra Kolenkow wrote her doctoral dissertation at Harvard on

---

[15] *Die Apokalypsen des Esra und des Baruch in Deutscher Gestalt, mit Textvorschlägen für Esra und Baruch von H. Gressmann*, Leipzig: J. C. Hinrichs, 1924.

[16] Violet, p. LXXIV.

[17] Violet, p. LXXVIIff.

[18] Violet, p. LXXVII.

[19] Violet, p. LXXIV.

[20] A. Kolenkow, *An Introduction to 2 Baruch 53, 56-74: Structure and Substance,* unpublished dissertation, Harvard, 1971.

2B 53 and 56-74, i.e., on the vision of the waters and its interpretation. She tried to show that it was dependent upon material in 4E. She then concluded that said chapters in 2B were written to refute the view of the endtime contained in 4E.

Kolenkow has failed to produce a convincing case for the dependence of 2B upon 4E. Her evidence is not clear enough to support her conclusions. For example, she claims that the influence of Daniel 7 can be seen in the fact that the Messiah in 4E 13 comes from the sea, and that the cloud in 2B 53 also arises from the sea. She then claims that 2B had no reason to include this detail, and so must have been influenced by 4E. Examples of such reasoning in her thesis could be multiplied.

Although Kolenkow has not presented a compelling case for her thesis, much of her work along the way is useful. Her comments on the traditional nature of the review of history in 2B are the basis of some of my analysis of it in chapter two. In this case she is not tied to trying to prove dependence of 2B upon 4E. Instead she compares the review of history in 2B, 1 En 93, 91, and in the Life of Adam and Eve and sees a similar pattern in all three. From this she concludes that the author of 2B is using a pre-existent tradition which he has altered in specific ways. On this point she is on solid ground.

W. Harnisch[21]

In 1969, Harnisch published a study of 4E and 2B in which he stated that the two works are in basic agreement in their theology. Through close exegesis of selected passages, he shows that both were concerned to defend the idea of personal responsibility in the face of the kind of "skeptical wisdom" described by Brandenburger.[22] These ideas sought to excuse the human race from any guilt associated with sin because sin is a fate for all humankind.

In his treatment of 2B and 4E, Harnisch demonstrates that in both works one's future fate is determined by one's present relation to the Law. In developing this doctrine, the author of 2B places Baruch and Moses in parallel and substitutes an other-worldly reward for obeying the Law for

---

[21] W. Harnisch, *Verhängnis und Verheissung der Geschichte*, Göttingen: Vandenhoeck & Ruprecht, 1969.

[22] E. Brandenburger, *Fleisch und Geist*, Neukirchen: Neukirchener Verlag, 1968.

the this-worldly one offered by Moses, especially in Deuteronomy.[23] The author no longer looks for a restoration of the earthly Israel, but rather sees its reward taking place away from the earth.[24]

I agree with Harnisch on the points just mentioned. My exposition of the two ages in chapter three of this thesis will begin with a closer look at his exegesis, and will detail some of the points on which I disagree with him.

In general, there is a problem in his methodology, which results from his treatment of 2B and 4E together. Several times in his book he develops an idea on the basis of an exegesis of 4E, and then somewhat uncritically applies his findings to 2B.[25] The special example which I shall take up in chapter three is that of his characterization of the present aeon. Ideas which are at the center of 4E, such as the origin of evil in the world, are at the periphery of 2B. Not to recognize that is to distort one's reading of 2B.

Harnisch's approach also becomes problematic when he compares the similar framework of the two books, i.e., the extended conversations between the seers and God. In both books there is an element of the correction of the seer by God. All commentators have realized that in 4E the tension between God and the seer is more pronounced than in any other apocalypse. Harnisch and others have compared 2B to 4E with respect to this issue and have judged the level of tension between God and Baruch in the light of that found in 4E. As a result, insufficient attention has been focussed on this tension in 2B because it is less strong than in 4E. It is my hope that the following study will help to address this problem.

It is probably true that if Harnisch had carried out his own analysis of the literary structure of 2B alone, he would have integrated his analysis more satisfactorily into the views of the author and into the structure of 2B. In this Sayler is correct.[26] However, it was his decision to analyze 2B and 4E concurrently which interfered most with his interpretation of 2B. As is often the case, it is 2B which got the worst of the bargain in this endeavor.

---

[23]See chapter five of this thesis.

[24]Harnisch, p. 221.

[25]This is not to say that he does so in every instance. In fact, he sees that the basic questions that the books were written to answer are different in each case.

[26]Sayler, *Promises,* pp. 86-91.

P. Bogaert[27]

In 1969, Pierre Bogaert published a two-volume work on 2B. The first volume is an extensive introduction to 2B, taking in questions of manuscripts, authorship, date, etc. It also contains some detailed essays on the relation of 2B to rabbinic traditions, to the Paralipomena Jeremiou and other works, as well as on the theology of the book. A translation of 2B into French closes this volume. Volume two consists of a commentary on the translation.

In his review of Bogaert's work, Strugnell says: "Our major complaint is that, in certain sections of the exegesis, proper form-critical sensitivity, and concern for the relations of the finished document with the underlying traditional material, have not been shown."[28] To this I would add that there is little if any connection between Bogaert's analysis of the literary structure of 2B and his explanation of the book's theology. The result is that although many sections of the treatment of the theology are provocative, and although I agree with some of the conclusions, nonetheless the analysis of the theology is often presented as a matter of obvious fact. The claims of Bogaert are too seldom supported by the necessary exegesis of relevant texts, as are those of Harnisch, or by reference to his view of the general structure of the work as a whole, as are Sayler's.

In spite of the shortcomings just mentioned, Bogaert has made an invaluable study for readers of 2B. He has produced an accurate translation complete with a commentary which discusses translation problems. He has presented a fresh and intriguing discussion of the original language of the book.[29] He has considered at length possible rabbinic parallels both to specific ideas in 2B and to traditions such as that of the throwing of the keys of the Temple into heaven by the priests. He has defended the originality of the letter with a variety of cogent arguments. He has pointed to the necessity of reading the whole book with its *Sitz im Leben* in mind (the destruction of Jerusalem), rather than chopping it up as does Charles.

What is particularly interesting for us is that Bogaert discusses the eschatology of 2B. He deals with the frequent dichotomy between a national, messianic eschatology and a more transcendent one. He finds

---

[27] See footnote 2.

[28] J. Strugnell, review of Bogaert in *JBL* 89 (1970), pp. 484-485.

[29] Bogaert defends the notion that 2B was originally written in Greek. Volume I, pp. 353-380.

that the former is subordinated to the latter. We will have occasion to deal with the same issue in chapters three and four of this thesis.

A. Thompson[30]

In 1977, Alden Thompson published a study of the problems of theodicy raised and solved in 4E. In chapter three, he compares 4E and 2B with respect to their literary structure and ideas.

Thompson's primary interest is in 4E, as the title of his book indicates. For example, like Harnisch he underplays the correction factor in God's dialogues with Baruch because of his concentration upon the more radical tension between Ezra and God in 4E.[31] Further, he turns what is admittedly an important theme of 2B, i.e., the capacity of man to obey the Law, into the central thrust of the book.[32] In effect, he has used 2B as a foil against which to develop his interpretation of 4E.

G. Sayler[33]

The most recent major work on 2B has been done by Gwendolyn Sayler in a dissertation done under the supervision of G. W. E. Nickelsburg at the University of Iowa. This thesis is important as the first thorough attempt to correlate the literary structure of 2B with its meaning. Sayler has pursued this study under the inspiration of the pioneering work of Breech on 4E.[34] In the course of her study, Sayler has provided an encompassing interpretation of 2B as a whole, placing at the center the story of the gradual consolation of Baruch. The consolation first of Baruch, and then of the people by Baruch, takes place through a series of conversations between Baruch and God in which God proves to him that he is both just and powerful. This teaching quells the doubts which had been raised in the minds and hearts of the author's contemporaries because of the fall of Jerusalem.

In the main, I agree with Sayler's interpretation of 2B. My reservations about her work are mostly in the form of nuancing what she has had to

---

[30]A. L. Thompson, *Responsibility for Evil in the Theodicy of 4 Ezra,* Missoula: Scholars, 1977.

[31]Thompson, pp. 126 and 148.

[32]Thompson, p. 133.

[33]See footnote 13.

[34]E. Breech, "These Fragments I have Shored against My Ruins: The Form and Function of 4 Ezra," *JBL* 92 (1973), pp. 267-274.

say, and in going beyond it to investigate in greater depth the mode of argumentation of the author, as well as paying more attention to the specific ideas of the two worlds and the place of the Temple in the scheme of the author. Nevertheless, I concur in her analysis of one aspect of the story line itself, viz., the consolation of Baruch (which is something also observed by Thompson[35]).

Overall, Sayler's presentation suffers from the opposite of the deficiency which she herself has found in Harnisch. She accused Harnisch of not putting his detailed exegesis into the context of the book as a whole. Sayler, on the other hand, has talked a great deal about the book as a whole, but has neglected to supply her readers with enough detailed exegesis to make her explanation of 2B more convincing.

THE PRESENT THESIS

My thesis will combine aspects of Sayler's and Harnisch's work. Like Sayler, I believe that a general grasp of the structure of 2B is necessary to order all of its diverse elements in a way which is consistent with the intentions of the author. Like Harnisch, I feel that detailed exegesis of key passages is required in order to determine how the author has worked with pre-existent material and how he has adapted various ideas to his own purposes.

The sequence of chapters in this thesis is indicative of how I think the author used his material. He adapted the two-world concept to his own purposes by dwelling on the ontological difference between the two aeons, and then by locating the Temple and Jerusalem firmly in the present, passing aeon. He thereby relativized the importance of the fall of Zion. In this process, he made a strong case for the centrality of the covenant and its Law in the life, past and present, of the community. He adapted the covenantal idea by substituting eschatological reward for earthly prosperity as the blessing that went with the covenant. In so doing he not only criticized a certain type of mourning for the fall of Jerusalem, but also discouraged hope in a restored earthly city, proposed by some as a reward promised for covenant fidelity.

In chapter six I shall make some suggestions about the historical situation to which this analysis points.

---

[35]Thompson, p. 122.

2

Structure

The purpose of this chapter is to present a coherent structure for 2B. This is no easy task, given the length of the book and the wealth and variety of material which it contains. Nonetheless, it is only as a result of such work that the many ideas in 2B can be ordered correctly and the book interpreted in such a way that Baruch studies can contribute their fair share to the study of apocalyptic and to the study of the change in Judaism occasioned by the destruction of Jerusalem by the Romans in 70 C.E.

I have accepted the common division of 2B into seven parts. Since each commentator sees these sections slightly differently, it is necessary to make the boundaries of my sections clear. The chart on the following page compares my scheme with those of Sayler, Charles, Bogaert, and Thompson.[1]

As can be seen from the chart, my own division follows that of Thompson except that I include the long lament of Baruch (10:1—12:4) as the beginning of the second section.[2] Given this role for the lament, the structure of the five central sections of the book is quite regular. Each consists of a prayer or lament (which is really an indirect prayer) of Baruch, followed by a dialogue in which God frequently corrects Baruch,

---

[1]G. Sayler, *Have the Promises Failed?*, SBLDS 72, 1984, pp. 161-62; R. H. Charles, *The Apocrypha and Pseudepigrapha of the Old Testament*, Volume II, Oxford: Clarendon, 1913, pp. 481-526; P. Bogaert, *Apocalypse de Baruch*, SC 144, 145, Volume I, p. 62; A. L. Thompson, *Responsibility for Evil in the Theodicy of 4 Ezra*, Missoula: Scholars Press, 1977, pp. 123-124.

[2]This aspect of my division corresponds to that of Violet, *Die Apokalypsen des Esra und des Baruch in deutscher Gestalt*, Leipzig: J. C. Hinrich, 1924, pp. 213ff.

	My Scheme	Thompson	Charles	Bogaert	Sayler
I	1:1—9:2	1:1—12:5	1—5	1:1—12:4	1—5
II	10:1—20:6	13:1—20:6	6—8	13:1—20:6	6—20
III	21:1—34:1	21:1—34:1	9:2—12:4	21:1—34:1	21—30
IV	35:1—47:1	35:1—47:1	12:5-20	35:1—47:1	31—43
V	47:2—52:7	47:2—52:7	21—35	47:2—52:8	44—52
VI	53:1—77:17	53:1—77:17	36—46	53:1—77:17	53—76
VII	77:18—87:1	77:18—87:1	47—77	77:18—87:1	77

followed in turn by an address, usually by Baruch to the people, but in section two by God to Baruch. The vast majority of the direct and indirect commands which the book contains are found in these concluding addresses in each section.

There is a consistent movement within each of the central sections from Baruch's prayer to God's discussion with him to Baruch's instruction of the people. Since the book itself moves from the lament of Baruch over Zion, through its various sections, to the address to the Diaspora, the structure of the book as a whole is analogous to that of the individual sections.

The audience of the message given by Baruch becomes wider and wider until all of Jewry is included. The following chart suggests this. That the speech in section II is from God to Baruch emphasizes the divine origin of Baruch's exhortation, and also emphasizes God's correction of Baruch in that section.

> II. God to Baruch.
> III. Baruch to elders.
> IV. Baruch to his son, friends, and seven elders.
> V. Baruch to the righteous.
> VI. Baruch to the people, "from the greatest to the least."
> VII. All of Jewry.

The structure of 2B tells us how to approach it. Since the literary movement of the book is toward the instruction of the people, this instruction is a key to the book and can be used as a standard by which to interpret each of the smaller parts. Our method will be to look for connections between the prayer and the address which bind the sections together, and to analyze the address using the commands contained therein as organizing elements, and to apply the insights thus gained to the body of each section.

Taking a closer look at each section, we can see that each of them has as its core a specific command or set of commands. Furthermore, the direct commands are almost entirely confined to the addresses in 2B. The commands are therefore of special interest to us. Beyond this, it is important to observe exactly how other themes of each section are related to the commands in the addresses. This is an important key to an understanding of how the author organized his diverse material.

SECTION I (1:1—9:2)

1:1	NARRATIVE: God comes to Baruch.
1:1-2:2	God announces the punishment.
3:1-9	Baruch protests (based on Temple ideology).
4:1-7	God answers that the promises do not apply to the earthly Temple.
5:1	Baruch again protests that God's glory is thus affected.
5:2-4	God again answers that his glory is to all eternity.
5:5-7	Baruch and company mourn (NARRATIVE).
6-9	Destruction of the city.

Since section I does not share the structure of sections II through VI, it is not possible to analyze it in the same way as those sections. A detailed analysis of the structure of section I is to be found at the beginning of chapter four. The section begins with a prediction of the destruction of Jerusalem given by God to Baruch, and it ends with a narration of that destruction (chapters 6-9).

SECTION II (10:1—20:6)

NARRATION (10:1-5) Baruch goes to the gates of the Temple.

PRAYER of Baruch (10:6-12:5) In the form of a lament. He mourns over the loss of the Temple, and asks who will judge the deed.

DIALOGUE (13:1-18:2)

13	God answers that Baruch will be a witness at final judgment.
14	Various questions about theodicy by Baruch.
15	God answers in terms of the Law and the two worlds.
16	Baruch protests that one trapped in the shortness of this life cannot attain to the measureless world.
17	God eliminates the shortness of this time as a problem, using Moses and Adam as examples.
18	Baruch classifies men with relation to Moses and Adam.

ADDRESS of God to Baruch (19:1-20:6)

19:1-3	God recalls the Mosaic covenant ceremony as seen in Dtn 30.
19:4-8	God says that the consummation should now be considered because everything needs a consummation. He claims that he is the judge, and Baruch must stop being afflicted about the past.
20:1-6	The destruction of Zion was necessary so that God may come to visit the world.

In the introductory prayer (in this case a lament), the reader beholds the pain of Baruch firsthand. Baruch's suffering leads him to a desire for vengeance against the destroyers. He asks, "Who is the judge?" and proceeds to act like a judge himself by condemning and sentencing the enemies (chapter 12).

At the end of section II, God addresses Baruch (chapters 19 and 20). 19:3-4 is the command which forms the core of this address.

> Now regarding everything that is, it is I that judge, but do not take counsel in your soul regarding these things, nor afflict yourself because of those things which have been.

Here God claims that he himself is the judge. The whole section works as a correction of Baruch's position. His attitude is wrong. He is not to judge.

The fact that God is judge is seen against the background of the Mosaic covenant (19:1-3). The Mosaic covenant is therefore seen as a universal regulating principle. Baruch need not worry about who will be judge because God has already set up a system by which he will judge everyone, including Gentiles. The very heaven and earth which Baruch has asked to stop their activity in chapter 10 are the witnesses of this judicial process.

There is another correction of Baruch in that the section begins with the mourning of Baruch and ends with God's command to him to cease mourning (19:3-4). This helps to explain why section II ends with an address to Baruch by God.

In 19:5ff a further argument is adduced to persuade Baruch to forget about the present evils, and so to support the command of 19:4. All that really counts is the end of things. In this framework, since the earthly Jerusalem will not exist at the consummation,[3] the destruction is not quite the disaster that it is seen to be in Baruch's lament. In fact, in chapter 20, Zion holds back the consummation, and so must be removed. This helps to answer the first part of Baruch's lament.

The full impact of God's telling Baruch to look to the consummation is not apparent until the next section in which his view of the two worlds is developed. Nonetheless, we must notice that the author assumes his two-aeon view when he speaks of the consummation in 19:5. We thus have the sequence: a) exhortation to obey the Law; b) two-world theory supporting this exhortation. This pattern is also found in chapter 15, and elsewhere in 2B. This will become clear in chapters three and four.

---

[3]See chapter four of this thesis.

Now that we have established the thread connecting the introductory prayer and concluding address of section II, we must briefly sketch out the rest of the section to discover how it contributes to the message we have articulated. This brings us back to the end of the lament, chapter 12. Here Baruch assures the enemies that they will be punished. Within the context of the lament over the destruction of Jerusalem, it is natural to suppose that the destruction is the sin for which they will be punished. However, this boastfulness and prosperity is not explicitly related to the destruction of Zion. In fact, as I will show in the next chapter, this language recalls the problem of the prosperity of the wicked and the suffering of the righteous which is a topos of wisdom literature.

As the dialogue begins in chapter 13, this theme of punishment is continued—the enemies will be punished in the future, and then Baruch will be a witness against them because he has seen the destruction of Zion (13:5). What is striking here is that in this chapter, which follows directly upon Baruch's cry for judgment brought about by his longest and most eloquent lament over the fall of Zion, this specific concern is at least diffused, if not omitted entirely. It is their general sinfulness, and in particular their ungratefulness toward God which is the cause of their punishment. In essence, their sin is no different from the sin of the Jews which causes the fall of Jerusalem. This is part of the author's effort to draw his readers away from a preoccupation with the punishment of the enemies to a concern to dedicate themselves to the covenant.

Ch. 14 involves various questions of theodicy.[4] The first problem is that there will not be many survivors of the nations in the endtime to be judged. In the wording of 14:2 one can see a more general concern than merely that of the punishment of the destroyers of Jerusalem:

> And now I know that those who have sinned are many, and
> they have lived in prosperity, and departed from the world,
> but that few nations will be left in those times, to whom
> those words shall be said which You did say.

Although we still have "the nations" here, the more general problem of the prosperity of the wicked is really at stake. This fits well with our analysis of the rest of the section, especially in the next chapter of this thesis.

---

[4]See Harnisch, *Verhängnis und Verheissung der Geschichte*, Göttingen: Vandenhoeck & Ruprecht, 1969, pp. 79-87 and 180-188 on this passage.

14:4-19 presents three problems. The first is that the goodness of the righteous did not prevent their exile or the destruction of Zion. The second is that most people must suffer here, and still cannot look forward to eternal life, because they are sinners. The third is that this world remains, but the people for whom it was created must pass away.

God's answer in chapter 15 involves what are to be two major themes of 2B—all will be judged by the Law and are personally responsible, and the future world is where rewards will be given to those who are now obedient to the Law. In chapters 16-18, God's instruction of Baruch, it is shown that the shortness of this life is no obstacle to attaining the measureless world, because obedience to the Law is all that matters. This leads to a recital by God of the founding of the Mosaic covenant which is a way of making explicit what obedience to the Law means. (See chapter five of this thesis.) God thereby makes Baruch's questions irrelevant, without answering them each in detail. The author apparently wanted to dismiss a number of problems of theodicy raised by his contemporaries by putting them in the context of the two worlds.

Section II begins with Baruch's lament and ends with a command not to lament. It also plays down a desire for revenge against the enemies by depicting all individuals as under covenantal obligations and by depicting God as the judge exclusively. It does so by pointing away from the present painful situation toward the end of all things and the future world. In this process of correction of Baruch, the place of the covenant is central, really occupying 15:1-19:4, and making it clear that the way to the other world is through obedience to the Law.

SECTION III (21:1—34:1)

NARRATION   (21:1) Baruch goes to the Kidron Valley.
PRAYER of Baruch dealing with the corruptibility of this world as opposed to the immortality to come. This is focused by the typical question "How long?" (Chapter 21).
DIALOGUE (22:1-30:5)
22-23   God says that the end cannot come until the number of mankind is filled up.
24:1-2   God speaks of last judgment.
24:3-4   Baruch asks when it will happen.
25   God gives signs of the end.
26   Baruch asks about the length of the tribulation.
27:1-28:2   God speaks of the twelve parts of the tribulation.
28:3-7   Baruch asks about the fate of the incorruptible ones and about the location of the tribulations.

29:1-30:1   God answers that they will occur everywhere, and
                 then describes the messianic age.
30:2-5   God describes the resurrection.
31:1-2   NARRATION: Baruch assembles the people.
ADDRESS of Baruch to the people (31:3-32:7)
                 Followed by dialogue between Baruch and people
                 (32:8-33:3).

Section III of 2B falls into our scheme easily. It was common both in psalms of lament and in apocalyptic works to ask "How long?" In the prayer of this section (chapter 21), this question becomes the occasion for a long passage detailing the transitoriness of this world, and comparing it to the immortality to come.

The address at the end of the section (31:3-32:7) contains several commands. The first is in verses 4-5: "Forget not Zion, but hold in remembrance the anguish of Jerusalem. For lo! the days come, when everything that is shall become the prey of corruption and be as though it had not been." As in chapter 13 the fall of Jerusalem had become an illustration of the punishment of sin, here it has become an illustration of the corruptibility of all things.[5] Therefore, the address of section III is closely bound to the introductory prayer (chapter 21) which is devoted to a meditation on the corruptibility of all things.

In the prayer, the thoughts on this passing world (21:12-18) are combined with a look forward to future immortality (21:19-26). So also in the address the reference to the corruptible world in 31:5 is combined with a look to future deliverance from the final throes of this passing world.

> If you prepare your hearts, so as to sow in them the fruits of
> the law, it shall protect you in that time in which the Mighty
> One is to shake the whole creation. (32:1)

We should note here the thought progression from the corruptibility of this world to obedience to the Law and thence to membership in the future world (31:5-32:1). This speech is analyzed fully in chapter three of this thesis. The obedience of the people to the Law sets them apart from the corruption of which even the Temple is an example. This is clearly expressed even in the way 32:1 forms a contrast to what precedes: "but as for you . . ." (ʾntwn dyn . . .). Obedience to the Law will see one safely through the final throes of the passing of this world. Verses 2-4 then explain those throes, and verse 5 introduces a new command.

---

[5]See chapter four of this thesis.

> Therefore we should not be distressed so much over the evil
> which has now come as over that which is still to be. For
> there will be a greater trial than these two tribulations when
> the Mighty One will renew His creation. (32:5-6)

Again, as in section II, the distress of the people is criticized.

Since the question which introduces the section is "How long?", it is fitting that the author should include some material dealing in a more conventional way with this question. The author does this by using the idea that a certain number of people must be born and live before the end can come.[6] Chapter 24 gives assurance of judgment for all sinners, and the rest of the section up to the address is devoted to a kind of composite apocalyptic timetable.

Just as in section II the covenant was paramount, so here in section III the idea of the world as inherently corruptible is what provides us with the organizing thread of the section.[7]

SECTION IV (35:1—47:1)

NARRATIVE (35:1) Baruch goes to the Holy of Holies.
PRAYER of Baruch (35) in the form of a lament.
DIALOGUE (36-43)

36-37	Vision during Baruch's sleep. In effect, a communication from God.
38	Baruch asks for an interpretation.[8]

---

[6]Rev 6:11 and 4E 4:36 contain the idea that a fixed number of the righteous must be filled up. The shift from a number of the righteous to a number of all mankind is part of 2B's generalizing tendency (Charles, *The Apocalypse of Baruch*, London: Black, 1896, p. 45). It weakens the "we-they" opposition between Jews and Gentiles. For the idea of God weighing and numbering creation, see J. M. Myers, *I & II Esdras*, AB, Garden City: Doubleday, 1974, p. 175 on 4E 4:36; and D. Winston, *The Wisdom of Solomon*, AB, Garden City: Doubleday, 1979, pp. 234-235.

[7]Sayler (*Promises*, pp. 14-38) says that this section is dominated by the problem of the delay of the endtime. This is true. However, we will see in chapter three of this thesis that the idea of the corruptibility of this world is the author's major contribution to the traditional material found in this section. Thus it is important to see the central function of this concept in this section.

[8]This prayer is not the major introductory prayer to the section, but rather is required by the form: vision—request for interpretation—interpretation.

39-40	God gives the interpretation ending with the time of the Messiah who will reign "until the world of corruption is at an end."
41	Baruch asks who will be saved.
42	God answers that the covenant will be the deciding factor.
43	God tells Baruch that he will be taken up, thus setting the scene for the testament of Baruch (chapters 44-45).

ADDRESS of Baruch to the People (44-45) in the form of a testament.

Followed by dialogue between Baruch and the people (46:1-47:1).

Section IV begins with a lament over the destruction of Zion (chapter 35). Apparently Baruch has still not been convinced that his mournful attitude is wrong and must still be further corrected. To understand how the address of section IV is related to the lament we must observe that the address is in the form of a testament, and that chapter 43 provides us with the framework of the testament. There it is revealed to Baruch that he is to leave this world behind: "And you shall forget whatever is corruptible, and shall not again recall those things which happen among mortals." (43:2b) In chapter 35 we saw Baruch remembering and being in anguish over what has happened to the earthly Temple and in chapter 43 we see God telling him to forget all that because it belongs to the earthly realm which he is about to leave. With that, Baruch receives the direction, "Go therefore and command your people." (43:3)

The speech of Baruch in Chapters 44-45[9] is to the elders who have a teaching function within the community, according to 2B. The first Part of the speech (44:3-7) concentrates upon obedience to the Law as the way to salvation, with Zion used as an illustration of God's relentless justice. The second part (44:8-15) deals with the two-world schema. Formally, it is seen as a reason for the first part of the speech. In other words, the author adduces the two-world schema as a reason for the destruction of Zion and an incentive for obeying the Law. It provides a motivation for the people to obey. We again have the association "Law—two-world schema" which we found in chapter 15 and in chapter 19.

Chapter 46 is part of this passage, but it is formally separated from the speech in chapters 44-45. It is an appendix to the speech which again stresses obedience.

---

[9]For a fuller analysis of this speech, see chapter four of this thesis.

But only prepare your hearts, that you may obey the Law, and
be subject to those who in fear are wise and understanding;
and prepare your souls that you may not depart from them.
(46:5)

Section IV contains one of the book's two visions. The vision and its
interpretation describe the fall of the enemy of Zion. The interpretation
also includes a reference to the Messiah. The messianic age is said to last
"for ever," but is then limited in time: "until the times aforesaid are
fulfilled." (40:3) This is not necessarily a contradiction, in that to the
Semitic mind the phrase translated here "for ever" ($l^c lm$) can mean simply
"for a long time."

Our task is to determine why the author has placed this unit here. It
seems to serve two basic purposes. First, it assures the people that their
enemies will be punished, but in the messianic time. This messianic age is
not to last forever.[10] A limitation is put on it which comes from the idea
of two worlds: "until the world of corruption is at an end." (40:3)

Second, the author has used the introduction of this material to furnish
himself with an opportunity to talk about who will be saved and who not in
the last time. He says that relationship to the covenant is the deciding
factor. This will determine who gets to the other world.

SECTION V (47:2—52:7)

NARRATIVE (47) Baruch goes to Hebron.
PRAYER of Baruch (48:2-24) asking for mercy because of the weak-
                ness of mankind.
DIALOGUE (48:25-51:16)

48:25-41	God says that evil is totally evil, and therefore there must be a punishment for it, but there is also a reward for the righteous. One is responsible for one's actions, and the judgment is based on the Law, which all know.
48:42-47	In spite of his mention of Adam, Baruch also insists on personal responsibility.
48:48-50	Baruch addresses the righteous. (Apparently out of place here.)

---

[10]A. F. J. Klijn ("The Sources and Redaction of the Syriac Apocalypse
of Baruch," *JSJ* 1 (1970), pp. 65-76) considers all three of the messianic
passages in 2B to be unimportant to the ultimate purpose of the author,
since they never affect the addresses of their respective sections.

49:1-3   Baruch asks what shape people will have "in Your day."
50-51   God answers, giving fullest description of the fate of
         the righteous in 2B.
ADDRESS of Baruch (52) telling the people to forget the 'past, and
         not to waste time lamenting or looking for
         vengeance, but to prepare their souls for the
         future.

The prayer at the beginning of section V (48:2-24) lays great emphasis
upon the frailty of mankind. The address of Baruch at the end of the
section (chapter 52) is a series of direct and indirect commands which can
be broken down into these: (a) stop lamenting for the past catastrophe;
(b) look to your own salvation by remaining in the covenant ("prepare your
souls"); (c) "rejoice in the sufferings which you now suffer." We again see
themes which are familiar to us forming the core of Baruch's address.[11]

The author begins the section by pleading, on the basis of human
frailty, for God's mercy (48:14-19), and he ends it by demanding obedience
to the Law (51:4; 52:7). A logical transition between these two positions is
formed by the body of the section, which is in the form of a dialogue in
which God stresses the absolute nature of evil and of personal responsibility. This leads to assurance of reward for the righteous and punishment
for the wicked. This in turn leads to a detailed description of what will
happen to the good and the bad in the next life.

SECTION VI (53:1—77:17)

NARRATIVE (53:1) Baruch falls asleep.
VISION of the waters (53).
PRAYER of Baruch (54) for interpretation, stressing personal
         responsibility based on the Law. God's marvelous deeds are
         mentioned. Verses 21ff show that God is no respecter of persons.
DIALOGUE (55-76)
55   Angel corrects Baruch, this time on his fear.
56-74   Angel interprets the vision. Angel reviews history
                  from Adam to the Messiah. The theme is that sin
                  brings punishment. The fate of Zion depends upon
                  the actions of the people living within it.
75   Baruch's reaction to the vision and
                  interpretation, culminating in a covenant-related
                  section (vv 7-8).

---

[11]This speech is lacking its usual narrative introduction. Charles
(APOT, p. 507) sees 48:48-50, 52:5-7, and 54:16-18 as fragments of one
original address. This would make a great deal of sense.

76   The angel tells Baruch to ascend the mountain
                before he leaves the earth, just as Moses did in
                Dtn.
ADDRESS of Baruch (77:1-10) in the form of a covenant renewal
                (see chapter five).
Followed by the response of the people: they ratify the the
covenant, and protest his departure. He again turns them toward
the Law.
77:17-26   is the eagle episode, which is a transition
                between 2B 1-77 and the letter in chapters 78-87.

Section VI contains a lengthy review of history. The section opens with
a vision which is a symbolic representation of the course of all history.
Then comes the accustomed introductory prayer. Baruch prays for an
interpretation of the vision. Key verses are 54:4-6.

> You reveal to those who fear You what is prepared for them,
> that thenceforth they may be comforted. You show great acts
> to those who know not; You break up the enclosure of those
> who are ignorant, and light up what is dark, and reveal what
> is hidden to the pure, who in faith have submitted themselves
> to You and Your Law. You have shown to Your servant this
> vision; reveal to me also its interpretation.

God's great acts in history are to be revealed to Baruch and this is meant
as a consolation for him and the people. The author shows that in each
period of history the fate of Jerusalem and more generally the goodness
or badness of each period depends entirely upon the behavior of the people
living in it, just as in 77:3-10 his position is that the fate of Zion depends
upon the action of the people. God's acts consist of the punishment of the
wicked and the reward of the righteous. The revelation of this truth
throughout history is a lighting up of what is dark for the readers. It is an
illumination of the meaning of history. Such a meaning for history is
indeed a comfort for the ones who fear God, because it assures them of an
ultimate reward, and of God's justice and power.[12] Thus assured, they can
reaffirm their devotion to the covenant.

This brings us to the address of Baruch to all of the people, "from the
greatest to the least." (77:1) Within this short speech there is a brief
review of Israel's history in terms of the covenant.

---

[12]See Sayler, *Promises,* pp. 14-38.

> For to you and your fathers the Lord gave a law more excellent than to all peoples. But because your brethren transgressed the commandments of the Most High, He brought vengeance upon you and upon them, and He spared not the former, and the latter also He gave into captivity; and He left not a residue of them, but behold! you are here with me. (77:3-5)

The recent history of Israel is therefore put into the same framework as the review of history. We now get a conditional sentence which is equivalent to a command to the people.

> If, therefore, you direct your ways aright, you also shall not depart as your brethren departed, but they shall come to you. (77:6)

Then the above admonition is reinforced by forcing the people to again consider the fall of Jerusalem, not from the point of view of the Temple ideology which has already been refuted several times in the book, but as proof that the covenant curses and blessings are valid. The fate of the Temple depended upon the behavior of the people, in 70 C.E., as well as throughout history.

> Have you not seen here what has befallen Zion? Or do you perchance think that the place had sinned, and that on this account it was overthrown? Or that the land had wrought foolishness, and that therefore it was delivered up? Know you not that on account of you who did sin that which sinned not was overthrown, and on account of those who wrought wickedly that which wrought not foolishness was delivered up to its enemies? (77:8-10)

The response of the people is to recall all that God has done for them, i.e., his mighty works. We should remember that the prayer at the beginning of the section has asked for an interpretation of the vision, representing history, which is based upon the fact that God reveals his "great acts" and thereby reveals what is not known and lights up the dark. There is therefore a common thread connecting the initial prayer and the final address which helps us to see the message contained in the body of the section. Looking at history correctly reveals God's justice and therefore is a consolation to those who obey the Law.

SECTION VII (77:18—87:1)

NARRATION (77:18-26) Baruch commissions the eagle to carry the letter.

LETTER of Baruch to the diaspora tribes.

78	Introduction, embodying the deuteronomistic schema.
79-80	Depiction of the fall of Jerusalem with emphasis on the fall of the Temple as judged by the deuteronomistic schema.
81	Baruch prays in lament and asks "How long?"
82-83	A poem against Israel's enemies which turns to a consideration of the hidden sins of individuals and culminates in:
83:4-8	Commands to look away from present distress and desire for vengeance to the future reward.
83:9-22	The preceding is supported by a poem about the passing away of this world.
84	Baruch renews the covenant which Moses established.
85	Support for all the foregoing found in the two-world schema.

The seventh section does not contain the structure shared by sections II through VI. It functions as a summary of some of the more important ideas of 2B.[13] As a summary, it is natural to suppose that it conveys the particular emphases of the author himself. If that is true, then we would expect to find special affinity between this section and the addresses of the central sections. In addition, just as we found the addresses to be constructed around specific commands, direct or indirect, it may be fruitful to look at the seventh section using its commands as the keys to its construction. If we are right in seeing the letter which comprises this section as playing a role within the book analogous to the role played by each of the addresses within their respective sections, such a methodology recommends itself.

Chapter 78, which begins the letter, indirectly commands the addressees (using conditional sentences) to recognize the present distress as brought upon them by their own sins. This would result in the kind of

---

[13]Bogaert, Volume I, pp. 76-77.

Gerichtsdoxologie described by Steck as one of the goals of preaching.[14] The people are urged to reject their own "vain error"[15] which brought them to such a pass. This introduction corresponds to the concern of the author to shift the focus of the people's attention away from speculation about the disastrous consequences of the fall of the Temple and away from any preoccupation with the punishment of its destroyers. The author now describes the destruction of the second Temple, his mourning over it, and God's communications to him in terms which recall chapters 1-77. This leads to a poem which assures the ultimate fall of the enemies (82:3-9). It is very important to notice, however, that the emphasis in this poem does not fall on the actual punishment of the enemies, but on the transitoriness of their prosperity. Thus it falls within the wisdom context already mentioned with respect to chapters 14ff.

The poem leads somewhat surprisingly into a consideration of private and hidden sins of individuals (83:1-3). This would hardly be appropriate if the author were really primarily interested in the punishment of the enemies. This impression is confirmed when we examine the next set of commands, contained in 83:4-9. There are two negative injunctions: "Let none therefore of these present things ascend into your hearts" (83:4) and "Let us not now look unto the delights of the Gentiles in the present." (83:5) Each of these negative injunctions is followed by a positive one, which are respectively, "But above all let us be expectant, because that which is promised to us shall come" (83:4) and "But let us remember what has been promised to us in the end." (83:5) The lesson to be drawn is, "Do ye therefore prepare your hearts." (83:8) This phrase basically means, "Stay in the covenant by obeying the Law."[16]

This last set of commands, turning the attention of the people away from desire for revenge and toward the preparation of their own souls for judgment, follows the movement of the preceding poem, which moves from the idea of the passing nature of the prosperity of the enemies to concern about hidden sins. Throughout the book we have seen such injunctions supported by a reference to the transitory nature of this world, and such is the case here as well. A litany illustrating the transitoriness of the

---

[14]O. H. Steck, *Israel und das gewaltsame Geschick der Propheten*, Neukirchen: Neukirchener Verlag, 1967, p. 355, entries under *Gerichtsdoxologie*.

[15]"Vanity" (*t⁽ywt⁾*) could be translated "forgetfulness" and so could come from a covenantal context. See chapter five of this thesis.

[16]See chapter five of this thesis.

present world is introduced by "for" in 83:10, making the entire litany (83:10-22) support the preceding commands.

This leads to a renewal of the covenant in which Baruch parallels himself quite explicitly with Moses insofar as they both are mediators of the covenant.[17] The commands in this section deal with keeping the covenant.

Ending his book in a characteristic way, the author supports all that has gone before with one more meditation on the two worlds, and upon the corruptibility of this one. Lest anyone miss the connection which he makes between the present catastrophe and this meditation, he puts this connection at the forefront of his closing remarks.

> 3) But now the righteous have been gathered
> And the prophets have fallen asleep,
> And we also have gone forth from the land,
> And Zion has been taken from us,
> And we have nothing now save the Mighty One and His
>   law.
> 4) If therefore we direct and dispose our hearts,
> We shall receive everything that we lost,
> And much better things than we lost by many times.
> 5) For what we lost was subject to corruption,
> And what we shall receive shall not be corruptible. (85:3-5)

We have here what is now a familiar pattern to us: description of the present evil times; exhortation to obey the Law, with the future hope in mind; all of this supported by a reflection on the nature of the two worlds. What is most striking here is something which has already become apparent to us and which we will investigate in more detail in chapter four of this thesis, namely that all which has now been lost, Zion in particular, was indeed part of this corruptible world.

This section ends, as we might expect, with several further commands to prepare one's soul, supported by reflections upon the transitoriness of this world.

CONCLUSIONS

Already our methodology has borne fruit. In concentrating upon the addresses at the end of each section, and then upon section VII as a

---

[17]See chapter five of this thesis.

summary of the author's main points, we have begun to evolve a coherent interpretation of 2B and of its structure. This is confirmed when we pay special attention to the direct or indirect instructions to the people.

In general, we have found that the intention of the author is to draw the attention of the people away from the loss of Zion and away from a preoccupation with the punishment of the destroyers of Jerusalem. Through references to the Mosaic covenant, and by paralleling Baruch with Moses, the author seeks to recall the people to covenantal obedience. In his use of the two-world schema, he manages to relativize the importance of the Temple and land in Judaism and to reorient the People away from a this-worldly attitude to an other-worldly one.

In the following chapters, I shall examine these themes in greater detail.

EXCURSUS:
THE ORIGIN OF THE LETTER

The following paragraphs depend upon Bogaert's evaluation of the arguments for and against considering the letter an original part of 2B.[18]

Objections to considering the letter an original part of 2B fall into two categories. First, although we have only one complete copy of 2B, and this copy contains the letter, numerous copies of the letter circulated independently of the book. Second, the form of the letter differs from the rest of the book. However, Bogaert deals effectively with each of these objections.

Bogaert shows that all of the copies of the letters which are not attached to the book are of one textual family. The copy attached to the book is therefore unique. He then compares the two types of the letter and concludes that the copy attached to the book is the earlier. This would make it appear probable that the letter was originally where we find it, and was later extracted from the context of the book.

Bogaert sees the letter as a simpler presentation of the view of the author, written so that the major points of the author will not be lost due to the possible difficulty of the form of an apocalypse. Our own analysis will confirm this. The form of a letter would therefore be no hindrance to considering the letter as originally part of the book.

---

[18]Bogaert, Volume I, pp. 67-72.

Recently the originality of the letter in chapters 78-87 of 2B has been challenged by Gwendolyn Sayler.[19] Her arguments are of two types. First, she claims, on the basis of her literary analysis, that 2B comes to a logical conclusion in chapter 77. However, if the epistle serves as a summary of the book as Bogaert asserts, then such an argument loses its force. Second, she tries to show that there are ideas developed in the epistle not found in chapters 1-77, and vice versa. Bogaert has already shown the close affinity between the ideas of chapters 1-77 and those of the letter. In the present thesis, it will become apparent that the letter is not an alteration of the viewpoint of 2B, but rather manifests the same viewpoint. I thus join the general consensus that the same person composed the epistle and chapters 1-77. I should caution the reader, however, that my analyses of chapters 1-77 do not depend upon whether or not one accepts this position with regard to the letter.

An Arabic Manuscript of 2B has now come to light.[20] The precise relation of this manuscript to the Syriac text from the Ambrosian Library has yet to be elucidated. Judging by the description of the Arabic given by van Koningsveld, it leaves the issue of whether the letter is original to 2B unresolved. The fact that the letter is indeed present at the end of the Arabic manuscript speaks in favor of the position of Bogaert and myself. This means that the two copies we possess of the whole of 2B (although the Arabic lacks 1:1-3:1) both contain the letter. On the other hand, van Koningsveld indicates that in the Arabic text the letter is introduced as a separate work. This last objection to considering the letter as original to 2B is not compelling, however, because even within the literary fiction of our author the letter must be conceived of as in some sense independent. It is seen, in the fiction of the book, as a quotation of a letter which Baruch wrote before he begins the narration which consists of 2B 1-77.

---

[19]Sayler, Promises, pp. 98-102.
[20]Van Koningsveld, "An Arabic Manuscript of the Apocalypse of Baruch," JSJ 6 (1975), pp. 205-207.

3

The Two-World Concept

HARNISCH'S TREATMENT OF THE TWO-WORLD SCHEME IN 4E and 2B

Much of Harnisch's work on 4E and 2B is devoted to an investigation of the two-world concept in terms of both its content and its function.[1] This chapter will consist of a brief review of his ideas insofar as they affect 2B, and an exposition of my own ideas in contrast to his.

Harnisch begins his presentation with the remarks of Vielhauer on the two-world concept. Vielhauer considers this concept one of the essential marks of apocalyptic. His description of it is a good place for us to start our study.[2]

> The essential feature of Apocalyptic is its dualism which, in various expressions, dominates its thought-world. Above all, in the doctrine of the Two Ages, in the dualistic time-scheme of world eras (*ho aion houtos* and *ho aion mellon*), the entire course of the world is comprehended. *This Age* is definitely detached from the *Age to come,* and therefore the words *"this"* and *"to come"* are not simply time divisions, but have a qualitative significance: *this Age* is temporary and perishable, the *Age to come* is imperishable and eternal. This idea first becomes explicit as a theory in the later Apocalyptic (4 Esd. and syr. Bar.), but it is in fact present already in the oldest Apocalypses.

---

[1] W. Harnisch, *Verhängnis und Verheissung der Geschichte,* Göttingen: Vandenhoeck & Ruprecht, 1969.

[2] P. Vielhauer, "Introduction" to chapter XVI ("Apocalyptic in Early Christianity") of Volume II of *New Testament Apocrypha,* E. Hennecke, ed. by W. Schneemelcher, Philadelphia: Westminster, 1964, p. 588.

Following Volz, Vielhauer sees this concept as existing alongside, but different from a "national eschatology" in which the restoration of Israel as a political state on this earth was envisaged. He claims that this latter view was held by the "rabbis."[3] For apocalyptic, the coming world was transcendent.[4]

Although Vielhauer's summary is useful, it suffers from the defect of treating apocalyptic as a monolithic entity. In fact, as he admits, the full apocalyptic "system" as he sketches it is not totally present except in 4E and 2B. Whether it is in fact implicit in earlier works is a matter for further investigation. Our task in this chapter is to determine how 2B develops and uses the two-world schema.

Depending upon Jenni and Sasse,[5] Harnisch demonstrates that before the Common Era, there is no clear example of the use of the word ʿolam to mean "world." Rather, it conveys a sense of time. 1 En 48:7 and 71:15 come closest to the meaning "world" but are somewhat unclear in meaning and uncertain in date. On the other hand, in Slavonic Enoch, the Testament of Moses, 4E and 2B, the New Testament, and rabbinic literature, the word ʿolam does have a spatial as well as a temporal meaning. The Testament of Moses could go back to the second century B.C.E.[6] It does

---

[3]Vielhauer's lumping together of the rabbis is problematic.

[4]Indeed J. J. Collins ("Apocalyptic Eschatology as the Transcendence of Death," *CBQ* 36 (1974), pp. 21-43) sees the transcendence of death as the distinguishing mark of apocalyptic eschatology. I would follow him on this, but would caution that the way this transcendence is expressed within each apocalypse is very important and could change our idea of precisely what function this transcendence serves in each work.

[5]Harnisch, p. 289. E. Jenni, "Das Wort ʿolam im Alten Testament," *ZAW* 64 (1952), pp. 197-248; H. Sasse, article on *aion* in *TDNT,* Vol. I, pp. 197ff, and article on *kosmos, TDNT,* Vol. III, pp. 867ff.

[6]J. J. Collins ("The Date and Provenance of the Testament of Moses," in *Studies on the Testament of Moses,* ed. G. W. E. Nickelsburg, Cambridge: SBL, 1973, pp. 15-32) argues against a date in the second century B.C.E., for one around the turn of the era. In the following article in that same collection ("An Antiochan Date for the Testament of Moses," pp. 33-37), Nickelsburg challenges Collins and argues for the second century date. In the third article of that same collection ("Some Remaining Traditio-Historical Problems in the Testament of Moses," pp. 38-43), Collins admits the strength of some of Nickelsburg's arguments: "I believe that the specificity of TM8 makes it probable that this work had an earlier, Antiochan stage. However, this history of the traditions involved,

not, however, contain the two-world concept. Apparently, the spatial meaning of ʿolam (which could well have resulted from the interplay between the Greek aion and ʿolam) is not clearly present until the late first century, E.C. This may explain the lengths to which both 4E and 2B go to explain the concept and to apply it to their problems.

Harnisch sketches the two-world schema as it appears in 4E and 2B and then discusses its function in these works. The problem with his methodology is that in treating both works together he sometimes tends to blur the distinctions between them. Our disagreements with Harnisch have to do mostly with the exposition in section B. II. of his book, entitled, "Die Geschichte als die unheilvolle Zeit dieses Äons."[7] It is especially there that he constructs a worldview based upon passages in 4E, and then too uncritically transfers this worldview to 2B.

For Harnisch, the two key passages for understanding 4E's view of this evil aeon are 7:11 and 9:18ff.

> For I made the world for their sake, and when Adam transgressed my statutes, what had been made was judged. (7:11)

> For there was a time in this age when I was preparing for those who now exist, before the world was made for them to dwell in, and no one opposed me then, for no one existed; but now those who have been created in this world which is supplied both with an unfailing table and an inexhaustible pasture, have become corrupt in their ways. So I considered my world, and behold, it was lost, and my earth, and behold, it was in peril because of the devices of those who had come into it. (9:18-20)

Harnisch then refers to Sirach 25:24 and Wisdom 2:23-24.

> From a woman sin had its beginning, and because of her we all die. (Sir 25:24)

> For God created man for incorruption, and made him in the image of his own eternity, but through the devil's envy death entered the world, and those who belong to his party experience it. (Wis 2:23-24)

---

and the interrelation between TM and the books of the Maccabees require considerable further clarification" (p. 43).

[7]Harnisch, pp. 106-142.

According to Harnisch, the author of 4E took these isolated statements of Sirach and Wisdom and from them built the apocalyptic worldview.[8] Whether 4E actually used these specific verses from Sirach and Wisdom is questionable, but it would seem that Harnisch is essentially correct. 4E has developed a full-blown description of two aeons based upon the cutting off of the present aeon from the creation. God's original creation did not involve death or trouble, but the present aeon is full of both. The dividing line, and cause of the discontinuity between the two aeons, is the sin of Adam.[9]

Harnisch is also correct in seeing the basic problem of 4E to be the discrepancy between present experience and the promises of the God who created the world and at the same time chose Israel.[10] This is the basis upon which Ezra challenges God in the first three sections of the book. The author's answer to this challenge is contained in the above passages. The split between creation and this aeon is not the fault of God, but of Adam. So, as Harnisch puts it, for 4E the world is pre- and post-Adam.

I have no problem with the analysis above. What is problematic is Harnisch's application of the insights gained from 4E to 2B. One obvious difference in the treatment of the theme of Adam as the originator of this troublesome aeon is that whereas 4E takes the idea and elaborates it, making it the solution of a central problem posed by his figure of Ezra, 2B does no such thing. On the contrary, the Adam theme is at the periphery of his thought. He leans rather toward considering the present world as inherently incapable of supporting human happiness, and as being essentially characterized by mortality. This will emerge from our exegesis of selected passages later in this chapter. First, we will follow Harnisch's arguments connecting 2B's ideas with those of 4E to serve as the background for our own exegesis.

The first passage which Harnisch adduces is 4:3.

> This building now built in your midst is not that which is revealed with Me, that which was prepared beforehand here from the time when I took counsel to make Paradise, and showed it to Adam before he sinned, but when he transgressed the commandment it was removed from him, as also Paradise.

---

[8]Harnisch, p. 117.

[9]For the Adam theme, see Brandenburger, *Adam und Christus,* WMANT 7, Neukirchen: Neukirchener Verlag, 1962.

[10]Harnisch, pp. 19-42.

The passage asserts that the city which was destroyed by the Babylonians was not the city which was the object of God's promises. The true Temple and city is in heaven with God. Harnisch simply states that these verses belong in the same context as the 4E passages quoted above, because the vision of the heavenly city is removed from Adam when he sinned.[11] The problem with Harnisch's analysis is that the removal from Adam of the vision of the city preserved with God, and the introduction of a sinful and corrupt era, are not necessarily equivalent. Furthermore, the author gives us no hint that he considers them equivalent in this passage.

The main purpose of 2B 4 is not to refer to the ejection of Adam from the Garden of Eden, nor to indicate the cause for this evil aeon, but is rather to draw a distinction between earthly and heavenly realities, as we shall see in the next chapter of this thesis. By so doing, the author relativizes the destruction of the earthly Temple as a matter of no ultimate consequence.

Next, Harnisch turns to 2B 56:5-16, the most important verse of which is 6.

> For when he transgressed, untimely death came into being, grief was named and anguish was prepared, and pain was created, and trouble was consummated, and disease began to be established, and Sheol kept demanding that it should be renewed in blood, and the begetting of children was brought about, and the passion of parents produced, and the goodness of humanity was humiliated, and goodness languished.

At first glance this may seem to support Harnisch's theory that for 2B Adam is the author of the present evil age, and that therefore 2B shares 4E's worldview *in toto*. Even he must admit, however, that there is no mention of Adam introducing sin into the world here. Furthermore, he is not even said to bring death into the world, but rather becomes the cause of "untimely death."

It must be recognized that chapter 56 belongs within a very specific context. It is the first of the "dark waters" in the review of history of section VI. It does occupy a special place as the first of the dark waters, but in another sense it is just one of several such periods. Also, 56:1-5 makes it appear as though God had complete and total control over all of history. The world, including its alternating periods, "was established according to the multitude of the intelligence of Him who sent it." Even

---

[11]Harnisch, p. 110.

the division of history into good and bad periods is the work of God (chapter 69). God's plan for history is unchanged by Adam's sin.

Harnisch says that in 2B 23:4, Adam as bringer of death is stressed.[12]

> Because when Adam sinned and death was decreed against those who should be born, then the multitude of those who should be born was numbered, and for that number a place was prepared where the living might dwell and the dead might be guarded.

Harnisch surely overstates his case in this instance. In this verse, the link between death and Adam's sin is taken from Genesis 3 and is not stressed by our author. It looks more as if 2B has used an idea current in his time in passing. The point of the context is that the end cannot come yet because the earth's allotted time has not run out.

In 2B 17:3, the phrase "cut off the years of those born to him" could well mean untimely death. Further, the fact that Adam's life brought death may allude only to his own personal death. 73:3 is evidence that for the author untimely death is all that Adam could be held responsible for. In the "time of My Messiah" (72:2), "no one shall again die untimely nor shall any adversity suddenly befall." (73:3)

2B 54:15 is a famous verse in which the author tells us that as far as he is concerned, Adam is basically irrelevant to the human condition.

> For though Adam first sinned and brought untimely death upon all, yet of those who were born from him each one of them has prepared for his own soul torment to come, and again each one of them has chosen for himself glories to come.

That this verse occurs in an introductory prayer makes it more likely that here we have the authentic opinion of the author. "Untimely death" is all that Adam can be credited with, and each individual is ultimately responsible for his own fate. The glorious life of the heavenly world is chosen by obedience to the Law, and therefore, as chapter 17 claims, length of life does not even matter.

To sum up this part of this chapter, it should be emphasized that 4E and 2B sound quite different, and are confronting distinct problems. 4E is obsessed with the problem of the source of evil in the world. It is dealing

---

[12]Harnisch, p. 115.

with theodicy. The rebellious Ezra challenges God directly. In response, Uriel insists that evil is a result of Adam's sin. Adam thus becomes the dividing line between a perfect creation and this troublesome world and is very important in 4E's argument. On the other hand, 2B is not really concerned with the source of evil. Thus, Adam's sin is not central in 2B.

The following pages consist of exegesis of passages in 2B which will illuminate the author's adaptation of the two-world scheme. We find in 2B two sets of eschatological language. One is related to the future new heaven and new earth of Isaiah 66:22, which also involves a restoration of Jerusalem (Isa 62:6-9). The other draws an ontological distinction between the two worlds which sees the present one as inherently corruptible. It is eschatological to the extent that at some specific future time, the present world will pass away altogether. Jerusalem and the Temple are part of this world, and so must also pass away necessarily. The present chapter of this thesis will investigate those passages which clarify the author's use of this latter eschatology. In the next chapter, we will examine how this is related to the more traditional eschatology as found in Isaiah.

2B AND THE TWO-WORLD CONCEPT

We first look at 19:6-8.

> (6) Because if a man be prospered in his beginnings and shamefully treated in his old age, he forgets all the prosperity that he had. (7) And again, if a man is shamefully entreated in his beginnings, and at his end is prospered, he remembers not again his evil entreatment. (8) And again hearken: though each one were prospered all that time—all the time from the day on which death was decreed against those who transgress —and in his end was destroyed, in vain would have been everything.

Charles mentions Solon's speech in Herodotus I, 32 as a possible parallel for this thought. The part of this speech which is most to the point is the following.

> Now if a man thus favoured dies as he has lived, he will be just the one you are looking for: the only sort of person who deserves to be called happy. But mark this: until he is dead, keep the word "happy" in reserve. Till then, he is not happy, but only lucky.

There is a much closer parallel, however, both in geographical situation and in language and thought. This is found in Sir 11:23-28.

> Do not say, "What do I need, and what prosperity could be mine in the future?" Do not say, "I have enough, and what calamity could happen to me in the future?" In the day of prosperity, adversity is forgotten, and in the day of adversity, prosperity is not remembered. For it is easy in the sight of the Lord to reward a man on the day of death according to his conduct. The misery of an hour makes one forget luxury, and at the close of a man's life his deeds will be revealed. Call no one happy before his death; a man will be known through his children.

The closeness in thought between Herodotus and Sirach is remarkable, especially concerning the reservation about calling anyone happy before his death. One could well ask if there is some dependence of Sirach upon Greek thought here, especially in view of his claim of having travelled and tested the wisdom of other nations in chapter 39.[13]

2B 19:5-8 and Sir 11:23-28 share: the references to prosperity (three times in Sir and four in 2B); language about "forgetting" and "not remembering" applied to the transition from adversity to prosperity or vice versa; the mention of death; the context of the judgment of God. 2B is certainly not quoting Sirach here. Even when one puts the obvious language problems aside, the parallelism between the two passages, although striking, is not close enough to justify such a conclusion. Nevertheless, it is no accident that the R.S.V. translation of Sirach and the Charles translation of 2B come out sounding very similar. The same reasoning is employed about the same issues.

Sir 11:28 is often cited in support of the idea that Sirach does not envision a future life.[14] One's immortality is identical with one's progeny. 2B is obviously saying something quite different. Most clearly in the case of the righteous, a future life after death is an essential element of his worldview. We thus see Sirach and 2B using the same arguments in two rather different contexts. For Sirach, the circumstances of a person's

---

[13]R. H. Charles, *The Apocalypse of Baruch*, London: Black, 1896, p. 34: "It was a familiar hellenic theme. Cr. Soph. *Trach.* 1-3; *Oed. Rex.* 1494-97; Eurip. *Androm.* 100-103, etc."

[14]For this issue in Sirach and Wisdom, see J. J. Collins, "The Root of Immortality: Death in the Context of Jewish Wisdom," *HTR* 71 (1978).

death will reveal his or her true state. For 2B, this revelation takes place after death. To make his point, however, the author of 2B is using arguments previously used in this wisdom work.

In the Book of Wisdom, the immortality of the righteous is used as a solution to the problem of the persecution of the good person by the wicked in this life. In describing this situation, Wisdom uses apocalyptic imagery in claiming that there is a future vindication for the righteous.[15] 2B seems in contact with the approaches of both Sirach and Wisdom. Like Sirach, it depends upon observation of one's environment and the inductive method to arrive at the conviction that a life cannot be judged until its end. Like Wisdom, there must be something beyond death for life truly to make sense. 2B has, however, avoided the position of questioning the reality of death which Wisdom took up (3:2), and thus stays firmly within the assumption of the wisdom tradition which based itself on empirical observation.[16]

Wisdom (chapter 2), Sirach (11:21-23) and 2B (14:1-3) are dealing with arguments used in the long debate over the fate of the righteous and of the wicked in the present world.[17] The practical result of this discussion which is desired by the author of 2B is that the readers turn their attention away from the sadness of the present time, and away from any longing for revenge, and towards the life of the world to come.

The Book of Wisdom is an interesting case of the penetration of apocalpytic materials into a wisdom work. 2B is usually considered an apocalypse, and in 19:6-8 we have observed a method of argument which belongs more properly to the sphere of wisdom. The general reflections about the necessity of a consummation are turned to the purposes of apocalyptic in that it is the consummation of the entire world which is at stake in chapter 20, and in that 19:1-4 deals with the judgment which God will carry out at the end on the basis of his covenant commands. What is important for us in this is that the author is using general observations about the nature of the world to prove the necessity of a consummation. True, these words do occur on the lips of God, but in our next passage, we shall see Baruch engaged in the same sort of observations.

---

[15]Wisdom 5:1-5. See J. J. Collins, "Root," p. 188.

[16]For this method, see J. J. Collins, "The Biblical Precedent for Natural Theology," *JAAR* 15 (1977), Supplement B, pp. 35-67.

[17]For a view which sees this as the central problem of 2B, see A. F. J. Klijn, "The Sources and the Redaction of the Syriac Apocalypse of Baruch," *JSJ* 1 (1970), p. 68.

21:4-25

These verses are the prayer of Baruch. It is the introductory prayer to section III. As such, they will tell us a lot about the main thrust of section III. As the division below demonstrates, this passage consists of three main sections.

I. (4) O You that have made the earth, hear me, that have fixed the firmament by the word, and have made firm the height of the heaven by the spirit, that have called from the beginning of the world that which did not yet exist, and they obey You.

(5) You that have commanded the air by Your nod, and have seen those things which are to be as those things which You are doing.

(6) You that rule with great thought the hosts that stand before You: also the countless holy beings, which You did make from the beginning, of flame and fire, which stand around Your throne You rule with indignation.

(7) To You only does this belong that You should do forthwith whatsoever You wish.

(8) Who cause the drops of rain to rain by number upon the earth, and alone know the consummation of the times before they come; have respect unto my prayer.

Ib. (9) For You alone are able to sustain all who are, and those who have passed away, and those who are to be, those who sin, and those who are righteous as living and past finding out.

(10) For You alone live immortal and past finding out, and know the number of mankind.

(11) And if in time many have sinned, yet others not a few have been righteous.

(12) You know where You preserve the end of those who have sinned, or the consummation of those who have been righteous.

II. (13) For if there were this life only, which belongs to all men, nothing could be more bitter than this.

(14) For of what profit is strength that turns to sickness, or fullness of food that turns to famine, or beauty that turns to ugliness.

(15) For the nature of man is always changeable.

(16) For what we were formerly we now no longer are, and what we are now we shall not afterwards remain.

(17) For if a consummation had not been prepared for all, in vain would have been their beginning.

III. (18) But regarding everything that comes from You, do You inform me, and regarding everything about which I ask You, do You enlighten me.

(19) How long will that which is corruptible remain, and how long will the time of mortals be prospered, and until what time will those who transgress in the world be polluted with much wickedness?

(20) Command therefore in mercy and accomplish all that You said You would bring, that Your might may be made known to those who think that Your long-suffering is weakness.

(21) And show to those who know not, that everything that has befallen us and our city until now has been according to the long-suffering of Your power, because on account of Your name You have called us a beloved people.

(22) Bring to an end therefore henceforth mortality.

(23) And reprove accordingly the angel of death, and let Your glory appear, and let the might of beauty be known, and let Sheol be sealed so that from this time forward it may not receive the dead, and let the treasuries of souls restore those which are enclosed in them.

(24) For there have been many years like those that are desolate from the days of Abraham and Isaac and Jacob, and of all those who are like them, who sleep in the earth, on whose account You did say that You had created the world.

(25) And now quickly show Your glory, and do not defer what has been promised by You.

The structure of this prayer of Baruch is as follows.

    I. Appeal to God as Creator (21:4-12)
    II. Interlude: Baruch reflects on this life (21:13-17)
    III. Baruch's requests (21:18-25)

Part I (vv 4-12)

This part of the prayer divides into two sections, 21:4-8 and 21:9-12.

The first section deals with God's creation of heaven and earth, and for the most part consists of traditional elements which can be found in the Psalms and elsewhere. The second section fits readily into the context of apocalyptic literature in that it credits God with knowing the number of mankind, with being the sustainer of those who were, who are, and who are to come.

Verses 4-8 are framed by the request by Baruch to God that he hear him. In verse 4 he says, "Hear me," and in verse 8 he says, "Have respect unto my prayer." Verse 7 is a complete, independent sentence. Aside from these three elements, the rest of the material in vv 4-8 is in the form of relative clauses, modifying the "you" of direct address. The purpose of the section is Baruch's appeal directly to God. The characterization of God in these verses gives a background to the appeal, and presumably should be suited to it.

The use of the theme of God as Creator is widespread in Judaism. The theme is usually adapted to its context and serves some specific purpose.[18] It is only when we have investigated Baruch's prayer as a whole that we can answer the question as to why the author has utilized creation material here. First, we must look more closely at the material itself for signs of its being adapted to the context in which it now is found.

The material is flanked by requests by Baruch for God to hear him, as was mentioned. The word for "prayer" in v 8 is b^cwt°. It is defined by Smith as "a request, petition, intercession, rogation."[19] This is not simply to be a hymn of praise, or a lament. Baruch intends to ask God for something. What that something is becomes clear in 21:20-26, to be examined below.

Most of the material in these verses is traditional, but some is not so

---

[18]In 1 QH 15 and Ps 8, God is portrayed as creator of all in order to contrast this with the lowly situation of mankind. In 1QH 15 this is carried out specifically in terms of God's knowledge and man's ignorance. In 2B 48 and 4E 8:20ff God as creator is appealed to in order to contrast his power with the puniness of mankind, and on that basis to beg for leniency in judgment. In Second Isaiah, God is depicted as creator in order to demonstrate that he is capable of a new creation. In Ps 74, God's strength in conquering chaos at the creation is called upon to deliver the people of the covenant from their enemies. In Ps 19, it is shown that the handiwork of the Lord praises him, as a model for the faithful worshipper to do the same.

[19]R. Payne Smith, *A Compendious Syriac Dictionary,* ed. by J. Payne Smith, Oxford: Clarendon, 1903, p. 50.

common in creation contexts. The first element of the latter material is God's ability to know of the consummation (vv 5 and 8). This supports Baruch's question about "How long?" (v 19). The second unusual concept is *creatio ex nihilo* which appears in v 4. This concept is found in Judaism before 2B only in 2 Macc 7:28.[20] In our passage it serves two purposes. First, it underlines the tremendous power of God. In this use it is another of the several statements about God as Creator in this passage which provide the rationale for appealing to him. He has the power, so requests should be addressed to him. Second, the concept tells the reader something about the nature of this world. It is not eternal. There was a beginning. Just as in ancient near eastern thought the abyss of chaos stretches below the order established by God, so here the threat of non-existence stretches beneath the existence of the creation. This is significant because much of the book is devoted to a description of this world which is meant to characterize it as of its nature contingent and transitory.

The phrase "from the beginning" occurs twice, in verses 4 and 5. This phrase is applied in two different ways. First, it is applied to the "world which did not yet exist." This application corresponds to the description of the creation of the world in the interpretation of the vision of the waters in chapter 56. There, the Mighty One creates the world with a fixed number of ages and sends it forth to run its course. In this application, the author is referring to the present, visible world. Second, God made "from the beginning" the "countless holy beings . . . which stand around Your throne." In other words, the inhabitants of the heavenly world are pictured here. Only God and his throne are eternal. All else has a beginning.

Having established God's past accomplishments and present power over the heavenly beings and all the world, the prayer moves on to assert that God is therefore the only totally free being. "To You only does this belong, that you should do forthwith whatever You wish." (v 7)[21] This freedom can be exercised both within the natural order, i.e., by causing rain or preventing it, and over the natural order as a whole, i.e., by determining the "consummation of the times before they come." On the basis of these reflections, Baruch asks God to "have respect unto my prayer."

Part Ib consists of verses 9-12. The section is again made up of statements about God's present power, but this time they refer not to the natural order as such, but to humankind, and in particular to sinners and

---

[20]B. W. Anderson, article on "Creation," *IDB*, Vol. I, p. 728.
[21]See Ps 136:6 and 115:3.

righteous people. God has an appropriate end prepared for each group. The source of God's power in this matter is that he alone is immortal (v 10). It is God's immortality which distinguishes God from mankind here. The idea of the mortality of humans occupies the rest of the prayer. It is important to notice that this idea is set in the context of the creation. All creation is creation *ex nihilo*. Therefore, all creation is of its nature contingent. Thus only God could be essentially immortal. Nonetheless, for the righteous there is a "consummation." Reference to this consummation runs throughout the book and finds its most complete treatment in chapter 51. The prayer of chapter 21 implies that the consummation is an overcoming of death.

Part II (vv 13-17)

In many ways this is one of the most remarkable passages in 2B. At this point Baruch seems no longer to be talking to God. This division departs from the previous style of constant reference to God's creative action and power, and turns instead to general comments about the lot of humans. These comments are discrete sayings, each one of which is introduced by "for" (*gyr*). The series follows immediately upon Baruch's reference to God's preservation of places for the good and the wicked, where the end of the good is termed a "consummation" (*šwlm'*). The whole passage, vv 13-17, supplies the reason for God's preservation of places for the righteous and the wicked. The reason is that a "consummation" is necessary because this life is ultimately unsatisfying. Thus the argument is the same as in 2B 19:5-8.

Verse 13 is very similar to 1 Cor 15:19, so much so that Charles suggests that it is "quoted from 1 Cor. xv. 19, or else both come from a common source."[22]

> For if there were this life only, which belongs to all men, nothing could be more bitter than this. (2B 21:13)

> If in this life only we have hoped in Christ, we of all men are most to be pitied. (1 Cor 15:19)

In spite of the closeness of these verses to one another in structure and diction, it would be rash to claim any direct literary dependence of one

---

[22]R. H. Charles, *The Apocrypha and Pseudepigrapha of the Old Testament,* Volume II, Oxford: Clarendon, 1913, p. 494.

upon the other. On the other hand, it is very possible that they both depend upon a common saying. Indeed, the verse in 2B could easily be used apart from its immediate context and still make a great deal of sense. The saying as it is found in 1 Cor, on the other hand, would not make sense apart from that context. If both verses go back to a common saying, 2B would seem to contain the more original form of it, since that form is capable of a much wider application than that found in 1 Cor.

A saying such as that found in 2B 21:13 would be very much at home in the context of the extensive wisdom discussions about the place of death in the life of the human race. In such a circumstance, this saying would be used as an appeal to experience to prove that there must be a life beyond which makes this life comprehensible. It is the expression in another form of what Wisdom 2-5 was trying to say.

Charles sees 21:14 as poetry.[23]

> For of what profit is strength that turns to sickness,
> Or fullness of food that turns to famine,
> Or Beauty that turns to ugliness.

This verse could also be detached from its context and still make sense. It is a comment on the worthless nature of all earthly goods. In its contempt for these goods it sounds Stoic. Nonetheless, it fits easily into wisdom reflections on the impermanent nature of prosperity. For its form, compare Mk 8:36: "For what good does it profit a man to gain the whole world and forfeit his life?" In Mark we also have a question (cf. Prov 17:16; 18:14; etc.) about the use of something. Bultmann terms this verse from Mark a *mashal*.[24]

In verse 15 there is a bit of a problem with the word "nature."

> For the nature of man is always changeable.

The word "nature" could hardly mean human essence. This would mean that human nature was constantly changing. This point becomes even clearer in the next verse where the "we" might indicate that even individual persons are examples of this changeability. Even evolution does not work that fast. However much weight of logic one wants to place upon the

---

[23] *APOT*, p. 494.
[24] R. Bultmann, *The History of the Synoptic Tradition*. Oxford: Blackwell, 1972, p. 81.

postpositive *gyr* in verse 15, it would appear that the author thought of verse 15 as flowing from verse 14. In this context, the author would be saying nothing more than that the lot of individuals always deteriorates. Wealth decays and beauty fades. "The nature of man" would then denote a person's concrete earthly existence, including such non-essential elements as social status and physical appearance.

Such a meaning for the "nature of man" could well fit 3:8 as well as 14:11, the other two occurrences of the phrase in 2B. In chapter three, the fall of the Temple calls into question the very earthly existence of humans, and in 14:11 the phrase is used in the context of a discussion of death and man's lack of control over it. The Syriac of Romans 2:27 uses the word *kyn'* to denote the physical sphere and the Syriac of Galatians 2:15 to speak of one's lot by birth.

Given the above interpretation, verse 15 is in effect a comment on verse 14. Likewise, verse 16 is merely an elaboration of the same thought.

> For what we were formerly we now no longer are, and what
> we now are we shall not afterwards remain.

Both vv 15 and 16 could easily stand on their own as independent maxims. The author could well have brought all of these sayings together to show the reason for v 17. Since life is so unstable, a consummation is needed. This second part of the prayer of Baruch ends with a verse which refers back to chapter 19, a passage which we have already discussed.

> For if a consummation had not been prepared for all, in vain
> would have been their beginning. (21:17)

In chapter 19 this verse occurs in the same situation as it does here. There the argument is that the consummation of each thing makes irrelevant its former history. Therefore, if a man dies happy, he forgets his former sadness. In our passage, the argument is slightly different. Because no earthly good lasts, a consummation is necessary.

Since 21:17 and 19:8 are so similar in wording and content, it would be natural to suppose that the author of 2B is adapting the same thought to two slightly different contexts. We have seen that a comparison of 19:8 with Sir 11:22-28 shows that the author could well be employing a reflection found in a wisdom context. In particular, 19:8 is found within an entire setting (19:6-8) which is connected to that sapiential context. At first glance, 19:8 seems closer to the original setting of the thoughts.

Note that the author again refers to "the beginning" in 21:17. This ties the verse into the creation section of this chapter (vv 4-8). It is likely that the author is therefore adapting the idea found in 19:8 to the context of chapter 21. The thought would now be that if no consummation had been envisaged for creation in the first place, then its beginning would have been futile.

If indeed the author is consciously fitting this verse into the setting of chapter 21, and if indeed "the beginning" of 21:17 is the same as that of 21:4,6, then this has important consequences for how we look at the author's two-world schema. In particular, Harnisch's impressive thesis must be modified. He claimed that the present aeon was cut off from the creation through the sin of Adam. We have already engaged him on this topic from the point of view of the use made of the Adam motif in 2B. In the present passage, due to the collocation of parts I and II of the prayer, we find the author employing reasonings about creation which make it appear as though from the beginning creation was as we now experience it—transitory and incapable of sustaining permanent happiness and goodness.

As 19:8 closes the author's argument about the futility of earthly prosperity, so 21:17 closes his argument about the passing away of all earthly goods. It is significant that the consummation in 21:17 and 19:8 refers to the end of an individual. However, 19:5 and chapter 20 put 19:8 into the context of the consummation of this entire aeon. Likewise, 21:8, 10, 19ff put 21:17 in this same context. We therefore move from the individual to the collective—an example of wisdom's inductive method.

In the next chapter we shall have occasion to suggest that the author of 2B picks up the slogans of those whom he wishes to engage and whose minds he wants to change. Here, it is possible that he has used a couple of sayings common in Palestine during the time after the destruction of Jerusalem. This would apply especially to 21:16.

> For what we were formerly we no longer are, and what we
> now are we shall not afterwards remain.

Alternatively, perhaps only the first part of this statement is taken from those whom he wishes to correct, whereas the second part is an example of his characteristic attempt to distract the people from the sorrows of the present to the changed and blissful conditions of the consummation.

Another pessimistic saying which may have been current in the author's time is 21:14.

For of what profit is strength that turns to sickness, or fullness of food that turns to famine, or beauty that turns to
ugliness?

Part III (vv 18-25)

21:18 introduces part III of Baruch's prayer. It interrupts the series of
gyr's established in verses 13, 14, 15, 16, and 17 by beginning with the
disjunction *ʾlʾ*. It switches from reflections about the nature of the world
to a direct questioning of God. The idea is stressed that everything comes
from God. This is accomplished by the parallelism between "regarding
everything which comes from Thee" and "regarding everything about
which I ask Thee."

Verses 19-25 deserve a very close reading. The author's purposes can be
discovered in them by trying to see in what ways they do *not* say what one
would expect them to say, but on the contrary say things which are somewhat unexpected.

The framework of the section is determined by the question "How
long?", a question familiar to psalms of lament.[25] What is surprising here,
given the fictional setting of the book in the period of the destruction of
the first Temple and the actual setting some years after the destruction
of the second Temple by the Romans, is that punishment of the enemies is
not explicitly stated. In fact, the three parallel phrases of the initial
question tend to blur precisely this issue of the enemies:[26]

(a) How long will that which is corruptible remain?
(b) How long will the time of mortals be prospered?
(c) Until what time will those who transgress in the world be
polluted with much wickedness?

Taken individually, each of these three elements addresses a different
question, but in the mind of the author they are all connected, and
together are meant to characterize the present age. According to this
reading, this age is characterized by transitoriness (the best translation of

---

[25]R. Murphy, "Psalms," *JBC*, Englewood Cliffs: Prentice-Hall, 1968,
Volume I pp. 572-573. See also his discussion of Ps 13:2-3 on p. 578.

[26]The word "transgress" here translates ʿ*br*. For this translation, see
Charles, *Apocalypse*, p. 41. Bogaert (*Apocalypse de Baruch*, SC 144, 145,
Volume II, p. 47) prefers "pass away."

the words from the root *ḥbl* throughout most of 2B[27]), mortality, and sinfulness. All of this is quite general. Nothing is said about the prosperity of the Gentiles or the Romans as such, nor about the bondage of Jerusalem or of world Jewry.

When in verse 20 Baruch asks God to bring about his promises, the content of these is left unspecified. True, those who ignore the "long-suffering" (*ngyrwt rwḥ*ᵓ) of God are the Gentiles in 12:4, but the word is used very generally in chapter 24 (verse 2, twice). There, God is "long-suffering towards all who are born, those who sin and (those who) are righteous."[28]

It should be noticed also that the word "prospered" (*mṣlḥ*) in verse 19 connects it again to chapter 19 where the same root occurs five times in four verses (19:5-8). Again, as in chapter 19, we are seeing the author in the process of putting the specific problems now being undergone by the community into the context of the general human condition, thereby relativizing the specific situation of Israel.

In 21:21, the destruction of Jerusalem is indeed mentioned. "Those who know not" that the destruction could take place only because of God's long-suffering are not specified as Jews or Gentiles. There is no good reason for us not to suppose that the author speaks of his fellow Jews here who have lost faith in God's power because of the destruction. The author is giving God control even over the destruction itself, as he does in section I of the book.

Finally, verses 22, 23, and 25 contain a long series of Baruch's direct petitions to God in the form of imperatives. The petition to "let your glory appear" (v 23) and to "show your glory" (v 25) employs typical theophanic language. See Isa 6:3-4 where God's appearance in the Temple is described as his glory filling the whole earth. In 2B 21, this petition is coupled with one requesting the abolition of mortality. Surely this is surprising given the setting of the book. One might expect the request that Zion be restored, or that the enemies be punished, or that the Messiah come, etc. Instead, we get a picture in which mortality itself, a characteristic of the present age, is the greatest evil, and therefore its removal is requested by Baruch. This is equivalent to a request that the present aeon pass away.

Before leaving these verses, we should notice the generalizing effect of v 24. Mortality is an affliction which touches each one individually and

---

[27]See Charles' translation of this word: *Apocalypse*, p. 41.
[28]See also 48:29; 59:6; 85:8.

without distinction. Specifically, it touches the righteous. This is a situation which has always obtained. Therefore Baruch bases his petition on the general world condition:

> For there have been many years like those that are desolate from the days of Abraham and Isaac and Jacob, and of all those who are like them, who sleep in the earth, on whose account You did say that You had created the world.

The evil from which Baruch asks to be delivered is not confined to his own historical time, i.e., it is not confined to the period of the destruction of Jerusalem, but is mortality, an integral part of the human condition. Implicit in this request is the belief that God has full control over death itself. It is a part of this world as he created it.

It is now possible to draw some general conclusions about this prayer of Baruch. It is a prayer in which Baruch is distressed not so much about the specific disaster involving the city and Temple of Jerusalem, but rather about the general condition of this age. What is good in this age does not last. Therefore, the age is inherently unsatisfying. If this age is all that there is, then "vanity" would be an apt word to describe it (*sryqwt*). Most characteristic of this age is death. It is this which Baruch sees as the greatest problem, and he asks the all-powerful God of Israel to remove it. Never once in this extended treatment of this age is Adam introduced. It is not explicitly denied that he is to blame for the regrettable condition of this age, but the prayer is constructed in such a way that it seems clearly implied that the world is as God himself created it, and that the consummation which he also created makes sense of humans' experience in the present.

A fascinating issue in chapters 19 and 21 is the part played by sapiential reasoning. Harnisch had already suggested wisdom influence because of this "meditative passage on the frailty of man" (21:9-12 and 48:12-17), the reflections about the actions of good and bad people (21:9-12; 54:14ff, 19, 21ff), and the description of humility (54:8-10).[29] His observations are supported by mine. This reasoning about everyday experiences is used to support and defend a belief in a future life. The same is true, in a somewhat different way, of the Wisdom of Solomon.[30] Also interesting is the fact that chapter 21 is in the form of a prayer of Baruch, and so is not

---

[29]Harnisch, p. 75, n. 1.
[30]J. J. Collins, "Root."

even a revelation from God. All this points to a somewhat ambiguous setting for our material. Although 2B is usually thought of as an apocalypse,[31] Baruch's prayer itself contains the solution to his own queries. That is because the way he puts the questions demands a certain answer. The lack of fulfilment of the promises (3:9) is due to the structure of creation as it was created. A future world has always been necessary. 4E's formulation of the problem, on the other hand, puts the blame on God for the lack of the carrying out of the promises in history.

Chapter 21, which occupies an important place in 2B as the introductory prayer to section III, is dominated by the notion of the ontological abyss between the two worlds. No restoration is mentioned.

Chapter 44

Chapter 44 is important as the concluding speech of Baruch at the end of section IV, and is in the form of a testament. 44:8 gives a basic principle which the following verses elaborate. It consists of a contrast between the two worlds.

> Because whatever is now is nothing,
> But that which shall be is very great.

The present world is not really real. (*mdm dhw' hš' l' hw' mdm.*)[32] The future world, on the other hand, is "very great" (*rb sgy*). The unreality of the present world is elaborated in verses 9-10. The present is that which "shall pass away," "shall depart," "shall be forgotten." The future world is the opposite. It "passes not away" and "abides for ever." The point of comparison here (note the verbs in verse 9—*'br* and *'zl*—and those in verses 11-12—*l' 'br* and *mqw'*) is that of transitoriness versus permanence. This is more ontological than ethical, even though the passage as a whole does include ethical elements. The author thus goes beyond those works which contrast the present and future worlds merely in terms of trouble versus bliss, dominance of the enemy versus the reign of the Messiah, unrighteousness versus righteousness, etc.

---

[31] J. J Collins considers it as an apocalypse. (See *Apocalypse: The Morphology of a Genre*, Semeia 14, SBL, 1979.) P. Hanson sees only the vision of the waters and its interpretation in section VI as an apocalypse because it is only there that we have an interpreting angel. (See P. Hanson, "Apocalypse, Genre," *IDB*, Supplementary Volume, pp. 27-28.)

[32] See the discussion of 48:29 below.

Chapter 44 is bound to the passages we have already discussed by its emphasis on the future consummation which shows the present to be nothing and the eternal world to be everything. Further, the mention of "prosperity" recalls the extended discussion of that concept in chapters 11-12, 19, and 21. Here, as there, the present prosperity of the wicked is transitory. The use of the root for "corruptible" (ḥbl, verses 9 and 12) to characterize this world unites the passage with numerous uses of the same root throughout the book. The word "to die" (kl mʾ dmʾt) connects 44:9 with the prayer of Baruch in chapter 21. Both see mortality as an essential trait of this world. As in 43:2, one will forget the present world once one attains the future one (44:9). The word "vanity" (sryqwtʾ) in 44:10 recalls the saying used in both 19:8 and 21:17, which we discussed in the context of the relevance of those passages to the two-world schema. The root bʿʾ ("to desire"—verse 11) is an important one in 2B, occurring some thirty times in the book. "Hope" (sbr) is another key word in 2B, as we will see later. These two words are crucial in that they are closely tied in with the attempt of the author to re-orient the desires and hopes of the people of his time to the future world.

Since this chapter is so central to 2B, it is not surprising to see various themes alluded to which occur throughout the book. These are now collected and used to support the exhortation implicit in 44:7. That exhortation to obey the law is bracketed by the testamentary framework, in which Baruch instructs the elders to teach the people the Law, thereby giving them life.

Sections Dealing with Anthropology

Scattered throughout 2B are statements which seem to suggest an anthropology based upon his version of the two-world concept. There are two classes of humans. One "belongs to" corruption (which is essentially nothingness), and one to life. To be sure, one is not predestined to either one of these groups. 2B is consistent in defending the idea of free will. However, given the fact that one actually chooses one or the other of the two worlds, one's nature then changes to conform to that choice. The following pages are devoted to a survey of the verses in question.

28:3-6

> (3)And I answered and said: 'It is good for a man to come and behold, but it is better that he should not come lest he fall. (4) But I will say this also: (5) Will he who is incorruptible

despise those things which are corruptible, and whatever
befalls in the case of those things which are corruptible, so
that he might look only to those things which are not corruptible? (6) But if, O Lord, those things shall assuredly come to
pass which You have foretold to me, so do You show this also
to me if indeed I have found grace in Your sight.'

Charles thinks that verses 4 and 5 are "an interpolation of the final
editor."[33] Further, "They are unreasonable and out of place in the presence of the sensuous picture of Messianic bliss which meets us in the next
chapter." In the previous chapter I explained that unlike Charles, who
assumes six or seven sources for 2B, I conceive of a single author working
with both traditional material and with material of his own invention.
While agreeing with Charles' perception of a certain discontinuity of vv 4-
5 with their context, I see this as an example of the author reworking
previously existing ideas with his own viewpoint. He does this not by fully
assimilating traditional material into his viewpoint, but rather by presenting the traditional view, and then subtly changing it by interjecting his
own slant on things at strategic points in the book.

If our understanding of the activity of the author is correct, then we
could well see 28:3 as a bit of traditional material, and verses 4 and 5 as
the author's subtle correction of it. We are justified in seeing verse three
as a traditional sort of comment. Expressions very like it occur both in 4E
13:16-20; 7:46-47 and the New Testament (Matt 24:22 and Mark 13:20).
Since Mark was written before 2B, it is reasonable to suppose that 2B
28:3 is not an original idea of our author. On the other hand, the root ḥbl,
very characteristic of our author, is used four times in verses 4-5.

We now focus on the phrase "he who is not corruptible," as contrasted
with "those which are corruptible." The root for "corruptible" (ḥbl) is very
frequent in 2B. It most often is applied to this world (21:19; 44:9; 85:13;
74:2; etc.). It is presented as an essential characteristic of this world.
Contrasted to this corruptible world, which is passing away, is the world
which is eternal, which does not pass away. The task of humans is to get
to that incorruptible world by following the Law.

In 28:5 we get the first application of the phrase "not corruptible" to
human beings. Corruptibility or non-corruptibility defined the essential
difference between the two worlds. Mortality was seen as part of this
corruptibility in chapter 21. Now this same word is applied more directly
to humans. Surely this is significant. It shows the author moving towards a

---

[33] *Apocalypse*, p. 51.

view in which there can actually be an essential difference between
humans. Of course, he does this well within the confines of the doctrine of
free will.

An interesting discontinuity between the traditional view represented
by 28:3 and verses 4-5 is that whereas verse 3 shows a concern about the
fate of people during the eschatological woes, verses 4-5 are more interested in the consciousness of the incorruptible one. Will he or she even
care about what is happening in the corruptible world? Will the fact that
he or she belongs to another realm cut off any connection with the lower
realm? Since the context is that of the eschatological woes actually
occurring, with the "incorruptible one" present, the question is one of
direct reaction to the events of the end-time. Later, when the context
becomes one of the future world as such, the question becomes one of
"remembering" or of "forgetting." In every case, the point is the radical
separation of the person who is entering the glorious realm from the
corruptible world.

42:7

> For *corruption* shall take those that belong to it, and *life*
> those that belong to it.

Here life and corruption are personified, and take those who belong to
them. This comes close to the language of Qumran in the distinction
between the children of righteousness, ruled by the prince of light, and
the children of falsehood ruled by the angel of darkness.[34] In 2B 42:7,
the words used with respect to people are those connected to the two worlds.
On page 53 I gave references for the application of the root ḥbl to this
passing world. "Life" is what is being presented by Baruch to the people in
the Law. Baruch claims that God's Law is life (38:2) and tells that in
teaching the people the Law he will give them life (45:2). Therefore, when
Baruch tells the people that he must leave them, they worry about where
they will be able to find one to teach the Law to them, which is in 46:3
put into synonymous parallelism with discerning the difference between
death and life. Baruch is thus paralleled with Moses, for it is he who sets
life and death before the people in chapter 19 by establishing the covenant. The author's discussion of mortality in chapter 21 shows that

---

[34] 1QS III. See Vermes' translation (*The Dead Sea Scrolls in English*,
Baltimore: Penguin, 1975, pp. 75-76).

mortality and corruption are essentially equivalent to the author, and that the passing of the dominion of one implies that the other also passes. In chapter 21 Baruch is praying for the future consummation, and this futurity of the concept of life is made quite clear in 57:2: "The promise of the life that should come hereafter was implanted" (referring to the time of Abraham).

The concept that people belong to one sphere or another is given further emphasis by the idea that one chooses this life in the present: "And as for those who before knew not but afterwards knew life . . ." (42:5).

The context in which 42:7 is found is a creation of the author. Chapters 41-42 say that one's attitude towards the Law will determine one's ultimate fate. This is a characteristic theme of 2B. Kolenkow claims that the notion of mingling versus withdrawing is also a theme of the author.[35] The words "time" and "consummation" are favorites of our author. Also, the characterization of the righteous as those who "believe" is shown to be one favored by the author in that he uses it fairly frequently, and in diverse contexts (42:2; 83:8; 59:2; 54:16; 54:21; 51:7; 54:5; 59:10; 57:2; 54:21).[36] The use of the word "to be subject" (eshtaphal of the root ⁽bd) is another way in which the author describes the righteous, as is evident from chapter 17, where it describes Moses.

In 42:7, the ontological difference between the two worlds has been expressed anthropologically. By their own choice, people belong to one or the other of the two worlds, and at the end this will become manifest.

Chapter 43

> (1) But do you, Baruch, direct your heart to that which has been said to you, and understand those things which have been shown to you; for there are many eternal consolations for you. (2) For you shall depart from this place, and you shall pass from the regions which are now seen by you, and you shall forget whatever is corruptible, and shall not again recall those things which happen among mortals. (3) Go, therefore, and command your people, and come to this place, and afterwards fast seven days, and then I will come to you and speak with you.

---

[35]A. Kolenkow, *An Introduction to 2 Baruch 53, 56-74: Structure and Substance*, unpublished dissertation, Harvard, 1971, pp. 109ff.

[36]See the discussion of the word "belief" at the end of this chapter.

Baruch's departure is an anticipation of the fate of all of the righteous, as becomes clear in chapters 49-51. He leaves the corruptible world and enters the incorruptible one. This transition is so definitive that Baruch will not even remember what he has left (43:2). This forgetfulness will also be shared by all of the righteous (44:8-9).

If we take the last two clauses of 43:2 as synonymous parallelism, then the world which is corruptible is identical with what happens "among mortals." This recalls chapter 21, the introductory prayer to section III, in which the petition is that mortality be removed forever. There, the present world is portrayed as that place "where mortals prosper." Here, the activity of this world is congruent with "those things which happen among mortals." The two worlds are being described in terms of a human quality—mortality. Baruch, and eventually all the righteous, are to escape from the sphere of mortality to one of immortality. This notion of passing from one world to the other is related to the common apocalyptic pattern[37] of the entrance of the righteous into the world of the angels (see 2B 49:10). The following is the description given of this process by Collins with respect to the Similitudes of Enoch (1 Enoch 37-71) "The human community of the elect and righteous stands in very close association with the angelic world and will be ultimately merged with it."[38]

2B is unique in the effort it gives to the description and contrast of these two worlds, specifically in terms which seem more ontological than ethical.

Chapter 48

Chapter 48 is the prayer introducing section V. As does the prayer of chapter 21, it concentrates upon God as the all powerful creator. *Creatio ex nihilo* is used here to underline God's might, and his total control over creation, as it is in chapter 21. Whereas in chapter 21 the image of the creator God led into a discussion of the nature of the present world, here it leads into a consideration of the nothingness of humankind: "Be not therefore wroth with man, for he is nothing." (48:14) Thus the point is a contrast between God and mankind.

The reflections upon the nature of man in chapter 48 certainly fit into the kind of "skeptical wisdom" traced by Brandenburger in the Hodayoth

---

[37] See J.J. Collins, "Transcendence."

[38] J. J Collins, "The Heavenly Representative the 'Son of Man' in the Similitudes of Enoch," in *Ideal Figures in Ancient Judaism*, p. 113.

of Qumran as well as in numerous other documents. Skeptical wisdom contrasts man, with his humble earthly origins, to God, both in terms of knowledge and of righteousness. A passage in 1QH IV illustrates this idea.[39]

> But what is flesh (to be worthy) of this?
> What is a creature of clay
>   for such great marvels to be done,
> whereas he is in iniquity from the womb
>   and in guilty unfaithfulness until his old age?
> Righteousness, I know, is not of man,
>   nor is perfection of way of the son of man:
> to the Most High God belong all righteous deeds.
> The way of man is not established
>   except by the spirit which God created for him
>   to make perfect a way for the children of men,
> that all his creatures might know
>   the might of his power,
> and the abundance of his mercies
>   towards all the sons of his grace.

In 2B 48, the Law plays the role that the spirit of God plays in 1QH IV, i.e., it lifts man out of his helpless and humble state.

> And the law which is among us will aid us, and the surpassing wisdom which is in us will help us. (2B 48:24)

Another helpful passage is Ps 78:38-39.

> Yet he, being compassionate,
>   forgave their iniquity,
>   and did not destroy them;
> He restrained his anger often,
>   and did not stir up all his wrath.
> He remembered that they were but flesh,
>   a wind that passes and comes not again.

Murphy asserts that this psalm evidences "considerable wisdom influence." As in chapter 21, we again see the author tapping into wisdom style

---

[39]Translation of Vermes, pp. 163-164. See Brandenburger, *Fleisch und Geist*. Neukirchen: Neukirchener Verlag, 1968.

reflections in order to pass a negative judgment upon this world. In this case, God corrects Baruch. Baruch has declared that the whole human race is nothing (48:14).

> Be not therefore wroth with man; for he is nothing. And take not account of our works; for what are we?

It is this appeal to God to pass over man's evil works because of his nothingness which God takes exception to in 48:26ff.

> You have prayed simply, O Baruch, and all your words have been heard. But My judgment exacts its own and My law exacts its rights.

The "but" at the beginning of verse 27 is the strong adversative ʾlʾ God has heard Baruch's words, but . . . . 48:27 recalls the words which God used in refusing the intercession of Baruch in chapter 5:

> And My judgment shall maintain its right in its own time. (5:2)

In both 48:27 and 5:2 God's judgment (dyny) insists upon its "right" (zdqh). The author's hand is clear here. His point is that one cannot hide behind one's lowliness as a human being when it comes to the judgment of God. This emphasis on individual responsibility is followed up in the description of the execution of God's judgment in 48:31ff.

> Therefore a fire shall consume their thoughts, and in flame shall the meditations of their reins be tried; for the Judge shall come and will not tarry. Because each of the inhabitants of the earth knew when he was transgressing, but My Law they knew not by reason of their pride. (48:39-40)

God insists on justice. His mercy is defined as the very giving of the Law.

> In You do we trust, for lo! Your law is with us, and we know that we shall not fall as long as we keep Your statutes. (48:22)

If such is the case, then what becomes of Baruch's statement that man is nothing? It is corrected by God at the beginning of his answer to Baruch.

> He that is corrupted is not at all; he has both wrought iniquity
> so far as he could do anything, and has not remembered my
> goodness, nor accepted my long suffering. (48:29)

A comparison of the Syriac of 48:14 and 48:29 shows how similar they are.

48:14   *lʾ hwʾ mdm hw*

48:29   *lʾ hwʾ mdm hw dmtḥbl*

In 48:14 Baruch says that man is "nothing." In 48:29, God says that it is
not mankind itself which is "nothing" but it is the one who does not
remember the goodness of God who is "nothing."

One must read these verses in the context of 2B's discussion of the two
worlds. 44:8-9 parallels "whatever is now" with "that which is corruptible"
and declares it to be "nothing."

mdm dhwʾ hsʾ lʾ hwʾ mdm (44:8)

ʿbr gyr klmdm dmtḥbl (44:9)

The association of corruptibility with nothingness is shared by 44:8 and
48:29. Chapter 44 says that the existing corruptible world is really nothing
at all. Chapter 48 therefore applies the characteristics of this world to
sinners and asserts that they are corruptible and are really nothing at all.
As the rest of section V makes clear, the righteous really belong to
another sphere altogether (chapters 49-51).

The close connection between the nothingness of this world and the
nothingness of sinners is also apparent in a verse already examined, 42:7.
There, corruption takes those who belong to it. The same holds true in
28:5. Note also the characterization of this world in human terms (mortality) in chapter 21.

> For all this multitude are going to corruption, nor is there any
> numbering of those whom the fire devours. (48:43)

The real punishment for not following the Law is to become part of this
corruptible world. In other words, although man is indeed now living
within the world which has been described at such length as corruptible
and passing away, it is his attitude towards the Law which will determine
whether he will stay in this world and pass away with it, or whether he
will escape it and live in the eternal world, thus effectively changing his

nature. God insists that the outcome of each life depends on the free choice of the individual to obey or to "forget" the Law.

Here again anthropology is tied up with the two-world concept. The interest in chapter 48 is primarily in anthropology. In particular, the fate of each of the two groups necessitates a two-world idea. This passage corroborates Gammie's close association between spatial and ethical dualism in Jewish wisdom and apocalyptic literature.[40]

Chapter 51

Chapter 51 contains the climax to the whole process of judgment, and constitutes a climax for 2B in general. 51:3 is especially noteworthy.[41]

> Also (as for) the glory of those who have now been justified in My law, who have had understanding in their life, and who have planted in their heart the root of wisdom, then their splendour shall be *glorified* in changes, and the form of their face shall be turned into the light of their beauty, that they may be able to acquire and receive the world which does not die, which is then promised to them.

Due to the understanding and wisdom which come through the Law, the righteous person is transformed (after the resurrection) into greater and greater glory. This transformation is necessary for this person to "acquire and receive the world that does not die." The righteous person goes from one sphere to another because he or she has wisdom in his or her heart which is equivalent to obeying the Law.

The sinners have stopped their ears so as not to "hear wisdom or receive understanding" so that they cannot now be transformed in glory and enter into the "world which does not die." Where they do go is rather vague. They are said to "waste away" (*šwḥ*), a word which is also used in 30:4 in the same context. They are to be tormented, and elsewhere fire is mentioned as their fate. It seems that in these instances the interest of the author is far more intense concerning the fate of the righteous. Indeed, this chapter represents the fullest presentation of the future world, and one is left in the dark about any place of torment.

---

[40] J. G. Gammie, "Spatial and Ethical Dualism in Jewish Wisdom and Apocalyptic," *JBL* 93 (1974), pp. 356-385.

[41] Note the closeness of this passage to 2B 44:13-14. In both, wisdom and understanding characterize the righteous.

The author anticipates the complete passing away of this world. He is trying to combine two different ideas. He has opted for denying any restoration of the present world, but has denied the wicked life in the world to come. As a result, he is left with a problem of where the evil will go. He does not solve this problem, but merely assigns them to the traditional fire. Elsewhere, he implies that they pass away with the world.

The fate of the righteous is described more fully in 51:7ff. There the entrance into the other world which is implied by their "splendor being glorified in changes" is laid out in greater detail.

> (7) But those who have been saved by their works,
>   And to whom the law has been now a hope,
>   And understanding an expectation,
>   And wisdom a confidence (belief)
>   Shall wonders appear in their time.
> (8) For they shall behold the world which is now invisible
>   to them,
>   And they shall behold the time which is now hidden
>   from them,
> (9) And time shall no longer age them.
> 10) For in the heights of that world shall they dwell,
>   And they shall be made like unto the angels,
>   And be made equal to the stars,
>   And they shall be changed into every form they desire,
>   From beauty into loveliness,
>   And from light into the splendour of glory.

Verse 7 characterizes the righteous. They are saved by their works; the Law is a hope to them; they are associated with wisdom and understanding. This description fits that found in 51:3 and 44:14. Furthermore, the words "confidence" (hymnwt⁾) and "hope" (sbr⁾) look forward to the description of the time of Abraham in chapter 57, as does the mention of "works."

> And the works of the commandments were then fulfilled,
> And belief (hymnwt⁾) in the coming judgment was then gener-
>   ated,
> And hope (sbr⁾) of the world that was to be renewed was then
>   built up,
> And the promise of the life that should come hereafter was
>   implanted.

The Law has become something which should point to an eschatological reality. Belief in a future life is now part and parcel of accepting the Law. It is no longer an option. It is only they who accept such a belief who will enter that world. As was plain in chapter 17, the point of the Law is being able to attain that which is measureless, in spite of living a short life.

The main clause of verse 7 is expanded in the verses which follow. Verses 8-10 concentrate upon the future state of the righteous. They enter the future world, and time no longer ages them. Their full membership in that world is symbolized by their being likened to the angels and the stars.[42] This develops 51:5. They now attain the beauty and loveliness (šwpr' and y'ywt') of which Baruch despaired in 10:17. The theme of glory, which implies membership in the heavenly world, is repeated in 51:10.

Again we see that the author's two-world concept has affected his anthropology. The resurrection is no longer a prelude to a renewed life on this earth. The earth is essentially flawed. The following is Stemberger's description of this situation.[43]

> Ort der Auferstehung is dann auch nicht mehr die Erde, auch nicht in gereinigter Form also die "neue Erde", sondern die jetzt unsichtbare Welt (51,8; cf. 4Esra 7,26), die unsterbliche (51,3).

This is so for the following reason.

> Die Welt ist wesentlich vergänglich, Ort der Drangsal, voll von Leid, da von Sünde befleckt (44,8-10). . . . Somit ist das Auferstehungsleben hier in das himmlische Paradies verlegt, nicht mehr auf Erden gedacht; und die Auferstehungsleib-Vorstellung wird ausdrücklich dem Ort des Auferstehungslebens angepasst (51,3).

In chapter 51, when God reveals to Baruch the reward that awaits the righteous, it is evident that he speaks from this other world which is to be

---

[42]For this theme, see Dan 12:3; 4E 7:97, 125; 1 Enoch 104:2; 2 Enoch 1:5; Matt 13:43. J. M. Myers (*I & II Esdras*, AB, Garden City: Doubleday, 1974, p. 239) sees the point in 4E to be the incorruptibility attained by the righteous.

[43]G Stemberger, *Der Leib der Auferstehung*, Rome: Biblical Institute, 1972, p. 90.

the scene of their reward. "This" world and "that" one suddenly change
their referents. In 51:16, "this" world now denotes the heavenly world, and
"that" world the world of corruption. In chapter 4, the heavenly city and
Paradise also are seen to exist presently in the presence of God. These
chapters agree in seeing the other world as identical with heaven, and not
with a renewed earth.

The Epistle

The Epistle to Baruch does not add much new to what the author has
already said about the two worlds. This is hardly surprising, if indeed the
Epistle is a summary of what the author has said in the main part of his
book. Three comments are useful.

First, the reflections upon the nature of the present world which we
attributed to a pessimistic wisdom context in chapter 21 are repeated
here in 83:10-21. Here they are more clearly placed in an eschatological
context. In fact, all of 83:4-21 is a speech in the "eschatological paraclesis" style to be explained in the following chapter.

Second, 83:9 is worth comment.

> For that which exists now, or which has passed away, or
> which is to come, in all these things, neither is the evil fully
> evil, nor again the good fully good.

One might almost assign this to a Platonic background. However, if we
recall our analysis of chapters 19 and 21 and the wisdom influence we
found there, it would seem more likely that we are dealing with the same
sort of context here. This is a general observation about the nature of life
to which one would expect Qoheleth could agree.[44] It also should be
noticed that we have our author's ubiquitous "for" introducing this statement, a statement which could well stand on its own as a maxim.

Third, chapter 85 assigns everything which the people have lost, including and especially Zion (verse 3), to this corruptible world. This relativizes
the importance of the loss of Zion and re-orients the view of the people to
the future world.

Further light can be shed on the author's view of the two worlds and its
place in his scheme of things if we examine the use of the word "belief" in
2B. Then we shall briefly comment on the place of the Messiah in 2B.

---

[44]We should note that this occurs in a context which deals with the
wisdom problem of the nature of earthly prosperity.

Belief

The root translated "belief" or "faith" (*hymnwt*) occurs some ten times in 2B (including once in the letter). Charles claims correctly that in 2B it means "belief." "Thus in lix. 2 those who 'believe' are opposed to those who 'deny'; in 42:2 to those who 'despise.' This is the meaning also in 54:5; 57:2; 83:8." In this same discussion Charles denies that in 54:21 the word can mean "believe." "Faith in this passage is contrasted with unrighteousness (ᶜwl = anomia). Hence we should take it here as equivalent either to 'righteousness' or 'fidelity to the law.'" He goes on to say that "In 54:16 the verb 'believe' may mean 'to be faithful.' But the context is doubtful."[45]

I would agree with Charles that in the cases he cites the best translation is "believe." I suggest, though, that the mere fact that "faith" is paralleled with "wickedness" in 54:21 is insufficient grounds for a change in translation policy there. Not to believe can indeed be considered wicked in many contexts. Plöger makes the case that Daniel was written in part to polemicize against those who refused to believe in a future life as this was presented in the author's circle.[46] Indeed, 59:2 and 42:2, mentioned by Charles, show that this could be true for 2B as well. In fact, the author's dwelling upon the two worlds and their difference would be beyond understanding unless there were some question of the acceptance of these ideas among his contemporaries. To simply remove 54:21 from this situation is somewhat arbitrary.

Additional support for this position can be found in chapter 57, the section of the review of history which deals with Abraham. Verse 2 is most important.

> Because at that time the unwritten law was named amongst them, and the works of the commandments were then fulfilled, and belief in the coming judgment was then generated, and hope of the world that was to be renewed was then built up, and the promise of the life that should come hereafter was implanted.

This juxtaposition of "belief" and "hope" anticipates 59:10, where the place of faith and the region of hope are revealed to Moses. Hope is a

---

[45]Charles, *Apocalypse*, p. 95.
[46]O. Plöger, *Theocracy and Eschatology*, Oxford: Blackwell, 1968, p. 21.

future-oriented word, and the "belief" here is in the future judgment. Likewise, in 59:10, faith and hope are seen in a context of future judgment, and in the mysteries of the heavenly world with angels, treasuries of light, voice of thunders, etc. In other words, belief is a future-oriented thing. As we have seen above, for 2B that makes it also a present reality, a turning of one's attention to the other world, which is identical with the heavenly abode of God.

A passage in which this same juxtaposition occurs, and which Charles neglected to discuss, is found in 51:7, the chapter which pictures the future state of the faithful.

> But those who have been saved by their works, and to whom the law has been now a hope, and understanding an expectation, and wisdom a confidence, shall wonders appear in their time.

The word which Charles translates as "confidence" here is *hymnwt'*, elsewhere translated as "faith." This is an illuminating verse, since the Law, understanding, and wisdom are all future-oriented. Yet in accordance with our remarks above about the present element of salvation, the people talked about here appear already to have been saved. Just as Law, understanding, and wisdom are in 2B synonymous, it is likely that we are to read hope, expectation, and faith here as also in synonymous parallelism. We are very close here to the terminology of Hebrews, where "faith" is essentially insight into the heavenly realities, and where Christ our hope has entered behind the veil of the heavenly sanctuary. As in Hebrews we probably have an author who believed in a Philonic-type universe using apocalyptic language to speak to a group whose apocalyptic disappointment was challenging their faith, so here we may have an analogous situation.[47]

The future-oriented content of the belief in 2B is stated most clearly in 83:8. "Do ye therefore prepare your hearts for that which before ye believed." Here it is clear that the content of the belief is the future life and the heavenly world. It is this which 2B is meant to inculcate. It is confronting a lack of belief on the part of its contemporaries. It makes the claim that true salvation lies in the future, for the world is of its nature unable to be the scene of this salvation. It speaks to people whose

---

[47]For this way of reading Hebrews, see G. MacRae, "The Heavenly Temple and Eschatology in the Letter to the Hebrews," *Semeia* 12, Missoula: Scholars, 1978, pp. 179-199.

idea of peace was the presence of God in his Temple, bringing prosperity to the land and to the nation Israel. It demonstrates to them that such a state of affairs was always at best temporary because of the transitory nature of this world. God is permanently only in heaven. By identifying heaven with the future world, 2B both relativizes the loss of the Temple and renews hope on the part of its readers. All of 2B seeks to console the people for the loss of their cultic and national center by proving to them that true hope lies not in the restoration of that center, but in the passing away of all of this world, including the earthly sanctuary, so that the future world can indeed be dedicated (ḥdt) by the entrance into it of God's chosen people, or, more accurately, of those people who have chosen that world.

The Messiah

Both Klijn and Bogaert have dealt with the place of the Messiah in 2B at some length.[48] Both of them reach similar conclusions. They each recognize that the three passages concerning the Messiah in 2B (29-30; 39-40; and 70-74) are inconsistent with one another. Both writers see our author as using traditional messianic material, belonging to what Bogaert calls a "national eschatology."[49] They see this messianism as subordinated to another kind of eschatology.[50] Bogaert calls it a more personal one, dealing with personal resurrection and judgment.[51] Klijn says, "The days of the Anointed One are a step in history in the direction of the incorruptible world."[52] Observing that in each of the three appearances of the Messiah in 2B, his reign is limited,[53] Klijn reaches the following conclusion. "In all these cases the author obviously tried to say that the times of the Anointed One belong to this world, the world of corruption. For this reason it has to come to an end to make place for the time of incorruption."[54]

---

[48]Bogaert, Volume I, pp. 413-419; Klijn, pp. 74-76.

[49]Volume I, p. 425.

[50]See the similar conclusions of M. Stone with respect to 4E in *Features of the Eschatology in 4 Ezra*, unpublished dissertation, Harvard. 1965.

[51]Volume I, p. 425.

[52]Klijn, p. 75.

[53]Klijn, p. 74.

[54]Klijn, p. 75.

Stemberger summarizes the order of events of the eschaton.[55]

> 2Bar erwartet ein messianisches Reich auf Erden. Wenn
> dieses zu Ende geht, kehrt der Messias in den Himmel zurück
> und dann erfolgt die Auferstehung: die Erde gibt heraus, was
> ihr anvertraut ist, oder auch die mit der Scheol fast identifi-
> ziert Kammern. Die Toten kehren wieder in ihrer ursprüngli-
> chem Gestalt, damit sie einander erkennen und von den
> Überlebenden erkannt werden. Dann wandeln sich die
> Gerechten, entsprechend ihrem neuen Aufenthaltsort, der
> himmlischen Welt, in Licht und Herrlichkeit, während die
> Sünder dahinschwinden. Ob die Sünder im eigentlichen Sinn
> auferstehen, ist dem Autor wenig wichtig; bedeutend ist nur
> ihre Bestrafung. Wo der Autor die Auferstehung in ihrer
> beseligende Kraft betrachtet, kann er darum die Sünder völlig
> übergehen.

CONCLUSIONS

In this chapter we have seen how the author of 2B places great emphasis upon the radical discontinuity between this world and the future one.
They are ontologically different. This view of his also affects his anthropology. That this emphasis is his own is confirmed by the observation of
the careful structuring of chapters 21, 44, 42, etc. and by the position of
these chapters in the structure of 2B.

The radical difference between the two worlds as seen by our author
leads him to see heaven as the place of the final abode of the righteous.
Heaven is permanent. The earth is corruptible. The identification of the
future world with heaven does not cause the author to abandon his temporal language. Although his view implies a vertical eschatology, i.e., a
passing from this world below to heaven above, nonetheless he retains the
temporal element: at some specific future time the world will actually
pass away and the righteous will be transported to heaven.

The introduction of the vertical element into the more traditional view
of a succession of worlds is a major step in the direction of gnosticism.
The influence of the author's eschatology upon his anthropology as examined in this chapter makes this view plausible. 2B would then be seen as an
important document attesting to a transitional period in the development
of thought from a more traditional to a more gnostic point of view.

---

[55]Stemberger, p. 96.

EXCURSUS:
PAUL AND SECOND BARUCH

I make no claim that there is any direct contact between 2B and Paul. However, there is some reason to think that there is a certain community of thought shared by the two. This emerged a little in our discussion of chapter 21, earlier in this chapter. It can be pursued with reference to chapters 48-51 as well.

The question in 2B 49:2 and that in 1 Cor 15:35 sound quite similar.

> In what shape will those live in Thy day? (2B 49:2)

> How are the dead raised? With what kind of body do they come? (1 Cor 15:35)

However, the context of Paul's question should be noticed. We said before that the context of Baruch's question was that of judgment. As Conzelmann claims, in 1 Cor 15, "Paul seeks to show that the resurrection from the dead is ontologically possible."[56] He is really answering the question "How?" It is asked by those who do not believe it is possible, as 1 Cor 15 shows.[57] To do this, Paul speaks of bodies of *sarx* and bodies of *doxa*. In using these terms, Paul manages to stress both the discontinuity between our existence on this side of the resurrection and on the other, and also the continuity of the self which undergoes this transformation.[58]

Paul does not speak of the soul being separated from the body at any point. As Conzelmann asserts, "He has no concept of the soul at all."[59] The discontinuity just mentioned is further expressed by Paul in a series of four antitheses contained in verses 42-44. Especially noteworthy is the first of these: "What is sown is perishable, what is raised is imperishable."

The thought of 2B is parallel to that of Paul at several points. Neither speaks of "soul" and "body" in the Greek sense. For both, there is a transformation of the self from a corruptible being to one which is incorruptible. For both, this involves a continuity of the self, but a radical transformation of one's essence. This involves for both a leaving of the realm of the flesh (Paul's term), a leaving behind of these "entrammelling members" (2B).

---

[56]H. Conzelmann, *1 Corinthians*, Philadelphia: Fortress, 1975, p. 281.

[57] Perhaps it is for this reason that Paul speaks only of the righteous in 1 Cor 15:42ff, and leaves in doubt the fate of the unrighteous.

[58]Conzelmann, p. 282.

[59]Conzelmann, p. 281.

The picture presented by 4E 7:78, 88, 100, on the other hand, is quite different. There, the soul is separated from its "mortal body." This takes place immediately at death, and it is unclear whether the later making of the soul "like the light of the stars" (7:97) involves a reclothing of them with some sort of body. It would appear that a more "spiritual" conception is at work here.

In his commentary on Second Corinthians, Barrett refers to 2B 51:3 to help explain Paul's conceptions.[60] It is instructive to look at 2 Cor 3:18 and 4:4-6 in this connection.

> And we all, with unveiled face, beholding the glory of the Lord, are being changed into his likeness from one degree of glory to another; for this comes from the Lord who is the Spirit. (3:18)

> In their case the god of this world has blinded the minds of the unbelievers, to keep them from seeing the light of the gospel of the glory of Christ, who is the likeness of God. For what we preach is not ourselves, but Jesus Christ as Lord, with ourselves as your servants for Jesus' sake. For it is the God who said, "Let light shine out of darkness," who has shone in our hearts to give the light of the knowledge of the glory of God in the face of Christ. (4:4-6)

There seems to be some sharing of language and concepts between Paul and 2B. Both discussions take place in the context of attitudes to the Law, both speak of an increase of glory in stages, both speak of light (compare 2B 51:3 with 2 Cor 3:7ff), both speak of knowledge or understanding in one's heart which causes the transformation into greater glory to occur, both speak of belief. The parallelism is continued in 2B 51:4 where the wicked are described as stopping their ears so as not to receive understanding. This is not unlike the veiled minds of the Jews in 2 Cor 3:14-15. In 2 Cor 3:16 an element of voluntary refusal to understand is being implied.

It has been argued that behind Second Corinthians there lies a controversy of Paul with gnostics of some sort. One need not subscribe to the idea of the existence of full-blown gnosticism in the first century C.E. to think that there were concepts in Christianity, Judaism, and Hellenism

---

[60]C. K. Barrett, *Second Corinthians*, London: Black, 1973, pp. 124-126 and 130-136.

which were inclining towards gnosticism. If that sort of development indeed underlies Paul's discussion in Second Corinthians, then it would not be out of place to suggest some such movement in the thought of 2B. The world is seen as inherently bad. Our connection to it through our mortal bodies is seen as a hindrance. Escape comes through wisdom and knowledge of some sort. 2B is not gnostic. Far from it. My point is to indicate tendencies which perhaps helped to make gnostic thought possible within Judaism. We should remember what good use the gnostics of the second century made of the letters of Paul.

4

Zion

INTRODUCTION

Second Baruch was written in the wake of the destruction of the Temple of Jerusalem[1] by the Romans in 70 C.E.[2] That destruction had raised profound questions for a religion and a nation which was centered upon its cultic place. Neusner puts it well.[3]

> When the Temple was destroyed, it is clear, the foundations of the country's religious-cultural life were destroyed. The reason is that the Temple had constituted one of the primary,

---

[1] The author makes no attempt to distinguish between the Temple and Jerusalem. The Temple defines the city. For example, section I begins with an announcement of the destruction of the city, but the description concentrates on the Temple. This lack of distinction persists throughout the book. For a similar view, see Sayler, *Have the Promises Failed?*, SBLDS 72, 1984, pp 18-38, n. 5.

[2] A date toward the end of the first or the beginning of the second century C.E. is commonly espoused. See Nickelsburg, *Jewish Literature between the Bible and the Mishnah*, Philadelphia: Fortress, 1981, p. 287, and P. Bogaert, *Apocalypse de Baruch*, SC 144, 145, Volume I, p. 258. For a discussion of other possibilities, see Bogaert, Volume I, pp. 270-295.

[3] J. Neusner, "The Formation of Rabbinic Judaism: Yavneh (Jamnia) from A.D. 70 to 100," *Aufstieg und Niedergang der römischen Welt*, New York: de Gruyter, 1979, *Principat* (II) 19, pp. 21-22. For a more detailed discussion of the day-to-day operations of the Temple and of its place in the life of the people, see S. Safrai, "The Temple," *Compendia Rerum Iudaicarum ad Novum Testamentum: Section One: The Jewish People in the First Century*, Volume II, ed. by S. Safrai and M. Stern in cooperation with D. Flusser and W. C. van Unnick, Assen: Van Gorcum, 1974.

unifying elements in that common life. The structure not only of political life and of society, but also of the imaginative life of the country, depended upon the Temple and its cult. It was there that people believed that they served God. On the Temple the lines of structure—both cosmic and social—converged. The Temple, moreover, served as the basis for those many elements of autonomous self-government and political life left in the Jews' hands by the Romans. Consequently, the destruction of the Temple meant not merely a significant alteration in the cultic or ritual life of the Jewish people, but also a profound and far-reaching crisis in their inner and spiritual existence.

The author of 2B resolved this crisis in three ways: (a) he showed that the earthly Temple which had been destroyed was not really the dwelling place of God's eternal presence; (b) he placed the earthly Temple firmly in this passing world; (c) he used the destruction as a proof of the deuteronomistic scheme of history (sin/punishment/repentance/restoration).[4]

The purpose of this chapter of the thesis is to examine closely the passages throughout 2B which deal with the Temple or Jerusalem and to attempt an interpretation of the author's purposes based upon this examination. Attention will be given both to individual statements about Zion and the Temple, and to the function of those passages within the larger section in which they are situated.

2B's preoccupation with the destruction of Zion is manifested by the fact that it is at center-stage throughout section one, and forms the basis for the letter of section seven. Furthermore, it is mentioned, or at least implied, in the instruction sections of every section from two through six.

INTERCESSORY BARGAINING FORM

2B 1-9 represents the author's modification of a form which is also found in Num 14:10b-25; 16:19b-24; Exod 32:9-14; Gen 19:1-19:28; and Ps Philo 12:4-10. We must now investigate this form and its function in each of the narratives in which it occurs, with a view toward discovering how 2B has used it and what its meaning is for him. The form, which we shall call an intercessory bargaining, consists of an interchange between God and an intercessor in which the intercessor tries to avert the wrath of God which is bent on destruction of his people. It has three parts.

---

[4]See chapter five of this thesis.

I. a. God makes his appearance.
   b. God announces the coming destruction as a punishment
      for the sin of the people.
   c. God makes an exception of the intercessor.
II. Prayer of the intercessor, in which he enumerates the
    reasons why God should not destroy his people.
III. God's response to the intercessor. He relents.

The chart on the following page shows how the passages cited fit this
form.

It is interesting to notice that the form, as contained in Num 14:11-25
and Exod 32:9-14, seems to be somewhat discontinuous with its context. In
Num 14:11, the glory of the Lord appears at the tent of meeting and asks,
"How long will this people despise me?" He then proclaims their destruction. Moses intercedes, and the Lord decides not to destroy the people,
but to deny the present generation entry into the land, excepting Caleb.
The episode is logically complete. The description of the forty years
wandering in the desert should follow. Instead, God makes a new beginning
in 14:26: "How long shall this wicked congregation murmur against me?"
He then predicts that this generation will die in the wilderness and will
not enter into the land, again excepting Caleb, as well as Jephunneh and
Joshua. This redundancy is easily avoided by skipping verses 11-25. 14:10
flows smoothly into 14:26. 14:11-25, however, are precisely the verses
which contain the form under discussion.

The case is the same with Exod 32:9-14.

> And the Lord said to Moses, "Go down; for your people, whom
> you brought up out of the land of Egypt, have corrupted
> themselves; they have turned aside quickly out of the way
> which I commanded them; they have made for themselves a
> molten calf, and have worshiped it and sacrificed to it, and
> said, 'These are your gods, O Israel, who brought you up out of
> the land of Egypt!'" (Exod 32:7-8)

One would expect that Moses would then descend and the story would
proceed. Such would indeed be the case if we now skipped to verses 15ff.
There would be no resultant roughness in the narrative. As the passage
stands, God again makes a new start in 32:9: "And the Lord said to Moses,
'I have seen this people. . . .'" Again, verses 9-14 comprise the form under
discussion. They interrupt the flow of the narrative in chapter 32.

This impression is fortified by the following observation. In 32:14, God
repents "of the evil which he thought to do to his people." Yet Moses then

	Num 14:10b-25	Num 16:19b-24	Exod 32:9-14	Pseudo Ph 12:4-10	2B 1-5	Gen 18:1-19:28
I a	14:10b	16:19b	24:15-18	12:4	1:1	18:1
b	14:11-12	16:20, 21b	32:9-10a	12:4	1:2-5	18:17-21
c	14:12b	16:21a	32:10b	12:2	2:1-2	18:17-19
II	14:13-19	16:22	32:11-13	12:8-9	ch 3	18:23-15
III	14:20	16:23-24	32:14	12:10	ch 4	18:26
II'					5:1	18:27-28a
III'					5:2-6	18:28b

descends and carries out a punishment on the people. Furthermore, in Exod 32:30ff, Moses proceeds as if the whole issue of the people's sin is still outstanding. In Exod 32:30 he says: "You have sinned a great sin. And now I will go up to the Lord; perhaps I can make atonement for your sin."

In view of the discussion above, we are justified on both formal and literary grounds in isolating Num 14:11-25 and Exod 32:9-14 and in considering them as self-contained units. Since the form has been inserted in these passages between the description of a sin and the punishment of its perpetrators, it happens that in each case the elements I, II, and III are followed by a description of the punishment. This is not really part of the original form, as is demonstrated most clearly by the discontinuity of the form with its context, and by the fact that the form as isolated is logically complete in itself. It ends with God's relenting, and so nothing more need be said. The punishment becomes important for 2B, however, because 2B 6-8 describes the punishment which ensues when the intercession of Baruch *fails*.

One must ask the question what function these forms serve in the contexts of Num 14 and Exod 32. Without the intercessory bargaining, the passages would both be narratives describing the sin of the people, and a punishment of the sinners only. The form adds the threat of God to totally destroy the people as a whole, innocent with guilty. In both cases, Moses protests that God should not destroy the people, adducing similar reasons in both instances. In Num 14, he protests that Egypt will hear that God has destroyed the people he has led out of Egypt, and will slander God's power. That would be contrary to God's promise that his power would be great. In Exod 32, the Egyptians will say that God's intent in bringing the people out of Egypt was evil, and he prays that God remember his promises to Abraham, Isaac, and Jacob. Thus, in both cases Moses' intercession involves appeal to God's fame and to his promises. God's fame and glory depend upon his fulfilment of the promises to Israel and upon Israel's well-being. Further, the references to the exodus undoubtedly evoke covenantal considerations. Moses' intercession is placed in this context.

Since God relents in each instance, he affirms the validity of Moses' arguments. The form thus serves to affirm the premisses upon which the intercession is made, and to show their power to preserve the chosen people. Moses is right. God's glory *does* depend upon his fulfilment of his promises to Israel in spite of their sin. "I have pardoned, according to your word." (Num 14:20) "And the Lord repented of the evil which he thought to do to his people." (Exod 32:14) At the same time as it demonstrates God's faithfulness to his promises, the form claims that Israel is sinful.

The maintenance of the relationship between God and his people is not due to the merit of the people.

In seeking a *Sitz im Leben* for such a form, one would do well to give the covenantal reference its full weight. Baltzer suggests that compositions such as Ps 106 could be used in covenant renewal ceremonies because of their confessional aspect.[5] At such ceremonies, God's faithfulness and the people's unfaithfulness were recalled. The antecedent history could be used to illustrate this, and therefore Ps 106 would be very appropriate. In the context of a homily given at such a ceremony, a narrative form such as we find in Num 14 and Exod 32 would be appropriate to stir the people to an attitude required by the service.

Num 16:20-24 exhibits the intercessory bargaining in its simplest form. Each element takes up a single verse. Again, at stake is the existence of the congregation. This time, the argument used by Moses is the injustice of destroying the entire people although only one has sinned. (Cf. 2B 14:4ff) Of special interest to us is that Moses is told to move away from the congregation so that God can destroy it. This is found with respect to Baruch in 2B 2. It is also found in Num 14 and Exod 32 in that God does not include Moses in the annihilation, but rather will make him a great nation.

Ps Philo 12 is the story of the molten calf taken from Exod 32. The author smooths out the discontinuities in the story but keeps the intercessory bargaining form. The second half of Ps Philo 12:4 reads, "Now therefore I will forsake them; and I will turn again and make peace with them, that a house may be built for me among them; and that house also shall be done away, because they will sin against me, and the race of men shall be counted as spittle." This is element I of the form. Ps Philo has expanded it by including a prediction of the future (as found in 2B 1:5), and connects the punishment with the disparagement of the entire human race (see 2B 3:8). Moses then descends to rectify the idolatrous situation. In element II, Moses reascends the mountain and begs God not to destroy Israel, the "vineyard." This middle element is particularly instructive. Although one might expect Moses to base his intercession on the rectification of the situation which he has just accomplished, he does not do so. Rather, he employs arguments reminiscent of Exod 32 and Num 14. He claims that if Israel is destroyed, then there will be no one to glorify God, nor will

---

[5]K. Baltzer, *The Covenant Formulary*, Philadelphia: Fortress, 1971, pp. 54ff.

anyone ever believe his promises again. Finally, in element III (Ps Philo 12:10) God says, "Behold, I am become merciful according to thy words."

By having Moses descend to rectify the situation before making his intercession, the author of Ps Philo gives the story a smoother flow, because he has avoided the redundancy of Exod 32. We no longer have Moses carrying out a punishment after God has been convinced not to act. Also, there is not a second intercession occurring outside of the form itself, as we find in Exod 32:30ff.

In Gen 18:1-19:28, the form is broken up by the insertion of the story of Lot and his visitors. After each of Abraham's questions asking whether God would save the cities if a specified number of righteous persons were found in them, God asserts that he would save the cities for that specified number. Any one of these answers corresponds to element III in our form, if only that number of persons could be found. It is this conditional nature of God's relenting which does not allow the form to resolve itself in the traditional three elements. Rather, it leads into a narrative in which it becomes clear that none of the inhabitants of Sodom and Gomorrah are righteous except Lot, who is only sojourning in their midst. Lot, having proven his righteousness by his hospitality and his protection of the mysterious visitors, is saved with his family. Here we have another instance of the righteous being removed before punishment is inflicted (as we saw in Num 16:20-24).

This exception of Lot from the punishment could correspond to element Ic. This element is more directly present, however, in the fact that Abraham, to whom God discloses his plans, is himself not included in the punishment.

Particularly interesting for us is that in Gen 18, elements II and III are turned into a dialogue between the intercessor and God. God promises to relent if the situation described in a conditional way by Abraham actually holds. The narrative about Lot's guests proves that it does not hold. There are no righteous Sodomites. This being so, God destroys Sodom and Gomorrah in Gen 19:24.

SECTION I OF 2B (1:1-9:2) AND THE INTERCESSORY BARGAINING

We shall now investigate 2B 1-9 with reference to the form of intercessory bargaining. We will find that the author uses this form, but also adapts it to his own purposes. Below is a chart showing how these chapters fit the form.

I. a. The word of God comes to Baruch. (1:1)
   b. God announces the punishment, and predicts the repentance of the people. (1:2-5)
   c. Baruch is told to leave the city, because his works and prayers protect it. (2:1-2)

II. Baruch protests, centering on the fate of Israel. (ch 3)

III. God answers, and repeats command to leave (I.c.). (ch 4)

II'. Baruch protests, centering on God's glory. (5:1)

III'. God answers and repeats command to leave. (5:2-4)

> In 5:5-7, Baruch and company mourn.
> In 6-8, the destruction is described.
> In chapter 9, Baruch and company mourn again.

In the following analysis, special attention will be paid to the assumptions behind Baruch's intercession, and the fashion in which God responds to him. At the outset, it should be noticed that Baruch's intercession fails. The form, which formerly had been used to validate the grounds upon which the intercession was based, such as in Num 14 and Exod 32, here is used to invalidate them. Baruch's arguments do not prevent the destruction of the city and the dispersal of the people. The author has reversed the function of the form and so powerfully counters a certain attitude embodied in Baruch's protests.

Element I.a. (1:1)

This is cast in the form of the communication of God to a prophet.

And it came to pass in the twenty-fifty year of Jeconiah, king of Judah, that the word of the Lord came to Baruch, the son of Neriah, and said to him . . . (1:1)

Element I.b. (1:2-5)[6]

(2) Have you seen all that this people are doing to Me, that the evils which these two tribes which remained have done are greater than (those of) the ten tribes which were carried away captive? (3) For the former tribes were forced by their kings to commit sin, but these two of themselves have been forcing and compelling their kings to commit sin. (4) For this reason, behold I bring evil upon this city, and upon its inhabitants, and it shall be removed from before me for a time, and I will scatter this people among the Gentiles that they prepare the Gentiles. (5) And My people shall be chastened, and the time shall come when they will seek for the prosperity of their times.

As in the other examples of this form, God now announces the impending judgment.

Element I.c. (2:1-2)

(1) For I have said these things to you that you may bid Jeremiah, and all those that are like you, to retire from this city. (2) For your works are to this city as a firm pillar, and your prayers as a strong wall.

The exemption of Baruch from the punishment constitutes him as the perfect go-between God and the people. He corresponds to Moses as an intercessor, for God also exempted Moses from the punishment which he announced in Exod 32 and Num 14 and used him as a mediator between himself and the people.

---

[6]In 1:4, the word *nt ꜙ b* is translated by Charles as "do good to" (*The Apocrypha and Pseudepigrapha of the Old Testament*, Volume II, Oxford: Clarendon, 1913, p. 481). This idea would be a bit strange here. Bogaert (Volume II, p. 10) suggests "to carry a message to." This is a possibility. Strugnell (in a private conversation) has suggested "prepare." None of these suggestions yields a totally transparent meaning, but either the one of Bogaert or that of Strugnell would make sense. I adopt that of Strugnell here.

Element II (chapter 3)

(1) And I said: 'O Lord, my Lord, have I come into the world for this purpose, that I might see the evils of my mother? Not so, my Lord. (2) If I have found grace in Your sight, first take my spirit that I may go to my fathers and not behold the destruction of my Mother. (3) For two things vehemently constrain me: for I cannot resist You, and my soul, moreover, cannot behold the evils of my mother. (4) But one thing I will say in Your presence, O Lord. (5) What, therefore, will there be after these things? For if You destroy Your city, and deliver Your land to those that hate us, how shall the name of Israel be again remembered? (6) Or how shall one speak of Your praises? Or to whom shall that which is in Your law be explained? (7) Or shall the world return to its nature (of aforetime), and the age revert to primeval silence? (8) And shall the multitude of souls be taken away, and the nature of man not again be named? (9) And where is all that which You did say to Moses regarding us?'

In verses 1-3, the author alters the form of the intercessory bargaining by inserting several verses in which Baruch reflects upon his own position and reaction to the announced destruction of Jerusalem. These verses stress Baruch's obedience to God, and also his acute sorrow over the destruction. These two facts about him make him the ideal mediator between God and people. He is not removed from before God as are the people. As a matter of fact, only he can go to the Temple ruins to receive revelation. On the other hand, his solidarity with the people is expressed by his sorrow.

These verses also establish Baruch's credentials in a different sense. Neusner has suggested that those who opposed the second war against Rome were accused of a lack of true sorrow for the ruinous state of the Temple. The example he brings forward is that of R. Joshua. In Avot de Rabbi Natan (A) 4, Joshua is seen lamenting over the destruction of the Temple. R. Johanan ben Zakkai assures him that the Temple is not necessary for atonement to be effected. Neusner explains this passage in the following way.[7]

---

[7] J. Neusner, *Development of a Legend*, Leiden: Brill, 1970, p. 114. Bogaert goes so far as to suggest tentatively that the author and R. Joshua were the same person (Volume I, p. 443). See also Neusner, *A Life of Yohanan ben Zakkai*, Leiden: Brill, 1962, revised 1970, p. 145. For more

My guess is that the issue to which this story is addressed is the effort to rebuild the cult by means of a new war. In his old age, Joshua opposed the gathering enthusiasm preceding the Bar Kokhba war. A story such as this one would serve to stress two principles. First, Israel does not depend on Temple cult for reconciliation with God. Therefore efforts to recover Jerusalem cannot be justified on the grounds of divine will. God wants no such thing. Second, by indirection, the story underlines the results of the first war. The Temple was destroyed once, and Joshua, among the disciples of Yohanan, was one of the mourners for Zion. He cannot therefore be accused of indifference, but rather must be followed because of his wisdom.

In presenting Baruch as a true mourner for Zion, the author insures that his work will be taken seriously by those of his contemporaries whom he wishes to reach. Those who are engaged in inordinate mourning for the destruction of the Second Temple would be more sympathetic to a figure who shared their attitude. As the author has God correct Baruch's attitude, that of his contemporaries is also corrected.

Baruch's acute mourning over the devastation is further underscored by his reference to Jerusalem as his "mother." This seems to have been an idea first used by Second Isaiah (49:14-21; 50:1; 51:18; 54:1) and which was current in the first century of the common era, as is evidenced by Paul's use of it in Galatians 4[8] and by its occurrence in 4E 10:7.

With the question at the beginning of 3:5 we rejoin the intercessory bargaining form.[9] "What, therefore, will there be after these things?" It is really *the* question of the entire book.[10]

Baruch's question concerns the consequences of God's intended

---

on the "mourners of Zion," see Bogaert, Volume I, pp. 135ff, and J. Klausner, *The Messianic Idea in Israel,* New York, Macmillan, 1955, pp. 438-439.

[8]See H. D. Betz, *Galatians,* Philadelphia: Fortress, 1970, pp. 247-248: "Paul takes up, no doubt polemically, a famous dictum of Jewish theology, 'Jerusalem (or: Zion) is our mother.'" In addition to the material from Second Isaiah, Betz refers to Str-B 3.573 and Pieter A. H. de Boer, *Fatherhood and Motherhood in Israelite and Judean Piety,* Leiden: Brill, 1974.

[9]Note the question form also in Num 16:22.

[10]W. Harnisch, *Verhängnis und Verheissung der Geschichte,* Göttingen: Vandenhoeck and Ruprecht, 1969, pp. 75-77.

course.[11] Implied in Baruch's questions which follow this basic one ("What, therefore, will there be after these things?") are a set of expectations about the results of the fall of Zion which are rooted in a certain view of the nature of Zion. It is this view which the author wishes to confront in chapters 3-5. We shall observe that this view could well grow out of a Temple piety nourished by the Psalms, and evidenced in such works as Chronicles and Ezekiel, and of which indications can be found closer to 2B's own time in Pseudo Philo. Farmer sees this type of ideology also implied in Josephus' description of the defense of the Temple in the Jewish war.[12]

"For if You destroy Your city, and deliver up Your land to those that hate us, how shall the name of Israel again be remembered?" This question assumes that the very existence of Israel is wrapped up in the physical survival of Jerusalem, and the independence of the land. The close association of the well-being of Zion and the survival of the congregation of Israel is in evidence in several psalms.[13]

The survival of Israel is also at issue throughout Ps Philo.[14] Especially interesting for us are the arguments which the author puts into the mouth of Moses when Moses is interceding for the people in the passage already discussed in the context of the intercessory bargaining form.

> (8) And then Moses went up into the mount and prayed to the Lord, saying: Behold now, you are God who has planted this vineyard and set the roots thereof in the deep, and stretched out the shoots of it unto Your most high seat. Look upon it at this time, for the vineyard has put forth her fruit and has not known him that tilled her. And now if you be wroth with your vineyard and root it up out of the deep, and wither up the shoots *from your most high eternal seat,* the deep will come no more to nourish it, *neither your throne to refresh* that your vineyard which you have burned. (9) For you are the one that is all light, and *have adorned your house* with precious stones and gold and perfumes and spices, and wood of balsam and cinnamon, and with roots of myrrh and costum have you

---

[11]Notice the similarity of this argument to the one of Moses in Num 14 and Exod 32. In all cases, the intercessor objects that the results of God's intended action are unacceptable.

[12]W. Farmer, *Maccabees, Zealots and Josephus,* New York: Columbia, 1956, pp. 84ff.

[13]Ps 74:2-3; 125:1-2; 126:1-6.

[14]For example, 9:3ff; 18.

strewed your house, and with diverse meats and sweetness of
many drinks have you satisfied it. If therefore you have not
pity upon your vineyard, all these things are done in vain,
Lord, and you will have none to glorify you. (Ps Philo 12:8-9)

The fictional setting of this speech is Mount Sinai, so it occurs well before
the entrance into the land and the conversion of Jerusalem into the center
of Israel. However, it uses language which seems to refer to Zion ("thy
throne," "thy house"). The image of the vine was used for Israel planted in
the promised land, and then uprooted from it in Isa 5:1ff and Ezek 19:10ff.
The mode of destruction envisaged here seems to be the removal of Israel
from its cultic center whence it derives life-giving water.[15]

"Or how shall one speak of your praises?" (3:6) This question seems to
imply that Zion is the only place where God can truly be praised.[16]

Another train of thought which may present itself here is that if the
destruction of Zion means the annihilation of Israel, then Israel will no
longer be able to praise God, and therefore he will not be praised at all.
This logic is present also in the passage from Pseudo Philo already quoted.

If therefore you have not pity upon your vineyard, all these
things are done in vain, Lord, and you will have none to
glorify you. (12:9)

It will be remembered that in Ps Philo 12, the destruction of Israel seems
to be accomplished by removal from God's throne and being uprooted,
probably from the promised land.

"To whom shall that which is in your law be explained?" (3:6) Strictly
speaking, this is also a connection of the existence of Zion with the existence of the congregation of Israel, or perhaps of the loss of the land with
Israel's survival. It also associates the Law with Zion and the land.[17]

---

[15]Note the strange imagery of the throne refreshing the vineyard. This
could be a combination of the images of Zion as God's throne and God as
the bringer of rain. On the other hand, Patai connects the water libations
at Tabernacles with the idea that "the deep" was directly accessible under
the altar on Zion. This interpretation is supported by the parallelism
between "the deep will come no more to nourish it" and "neither thy
throne to refresh." R. Patai, *Man and Temple in Ancient Jewish Myth and
Ritual*, New York: Nelson, 1947, chapter three, especially p. 86.

[16]See Ps 137:4; 48:9-10; 65:1; 102:21; 99:9, and Chronicles, *passim*.

[17]See Isa 2:3; Ps 19:7ff; 119:1ff; Lam 2:9; Sir 24; Safrai, pp. 865-866
and 896-898. See also Josephus, Ant IV 209-211.

"Shall the world return to its nature (of aforetime), and the age revert to primeval silence?" These questions point to a cosmic role of the Temple. The Temple is often associated with creation.[18]

In Pseudo Philo 9:3, a comparison is even drawn between the universe and the existence of Israel.

"And shall the multitude of souls be taken away, and the nature of man not again be named?" This connection of the existence of the Temple and the continuance of the human race surfaces also in Ps Philo, again in the context of the interchange between God and Moses within what we have termed the intercessory bargaining. There, it occurs on the lips of God.

> Now therefore I will forsake them: and I will turn again and make peace with them, that a house may be built for me among them; and that house also shall be done away, because they will sin against me, and the race of men shall be unto me as a drop of a pitcher, and shall be counted as spittle. (Ps Philo 12:4)

"And where is all that which you did say to Moses regarding us?" (3:9) Explicit reference to God's promises is found in Num 14 and Exod 32, as well as in Ps Philo 12:9.

> For even if you plant another vineyard, neither will that one trust in you, because you did destroy the former.

SUMMARY

We take a moment here in our analysis to comment upon the effectiveness with which the author of 2B is using the intercessory bargaining form. He has put on the lips of the intercessor, Baruch in this case, various objections to the destruction of the Temple and to the subjugation of the land to foreigners. These objections are based upon a Temple ideology which can be traced in the Old Testament, and in Philo, Josephus, and Pseudo Philo. The author shows that objections based on this ideology do

---

[18]See also Ps 46:1-7. Jerusalem is seen as the center of the world in 1 En 24 and 25, and in Jub 8. See especially Hamerton-Kelly, "The Temple and the Origins of Jewish Apocalyptic," *VT* 20 (1970), p. 3; Patai, pp. 54ff; W. D. Davies, *The Territorial Dimension of Judaism,* Berkeley: University of California, 1982, p. 2.

not prevent God from destroying the city. In this way the ideology is confronted and denied.[19]

Element III (chapter 4)

(1) And the Lord said unto me: This city shall be delivered up for a time, and the people shall be chastened during a time, and the world will not be given over to oblivion. (2) Do you think that this is that city of which I said: "On the palms of my hands have I graven thee?" (3) This building now built in your midst is not that which is revealed with Me, that which was prepared beforehand here from the time when I took counsel to make Paradise, and showed it to Adam before he sinned, but when he transgressed the commandment it was removed from him, as also Paradise. (4) And after these things I showed it to my servant Abraham by night among the portions of the victims. (5) And again also I showed it to Moses on Mount Sinai when I showed to him the likeness of the tabernacle and all its vessels. (6) And now, behold, it is preserved with Me, as also Paradise. (7) Go, therefore, and do as I command you.

Since Charles considers 4:2-7 an interpolation, he lets 4:1 stand on its own as an answer to Baruch's questions.[20] Charles sees the point of the answer of God in the "for a time" mentioned twice in 4:1. Indeed, this is an important part of God's answer. A glance back at 1:4-5 shows that it builds upon what God has already said. What 4:1 adds to this is the idea that this implies that the world must continue. The answer does not imply that the world will continue indefinitely. The preceding chapter of this thesis has demonstrated that this is not so. Rather, it refutes the idea that the destruction of the Temple signals the end of the world.

---

[19]The Temple piety described by Safrai (pp. 904-906) can also be found in the New Testament (J. Fitzmyer, *The Gospel According to Luke*, I-IX, AB, Garden City: Doubleday, p. 316; Bachmann, *Jerusalem und der Tempel*, Stuttgart: Kohlhammer, 1980, pp. 261ff). In the "synoptic apocalypse" one can discern the connection made between the world as experienced and the existence of the Temple (L. Gaston, *No Stone on Another*, Leiden: Brill, 1970, p. 12; N. Perrin, "Towards an Interpretation of the Gospel of Mark," *Christology and a Modern Pilgrimage*, ed. by H. D. Betz, Missoula: Scholars, 1974). The fall of the Temple naturally led to the kinds of questions we have before us in chapter 3 of 2B.

[20]Charles, *APOT*, p. 482.

Charles has omitted 4:2-7 because[21]

> . . . the earthly Jerusalem is here derided, and contrasted
> with the one to be revealed. In 6:9, Jerusalem though to be
> delivered up for a time, as in 4:1, will again be restored, and
> that for ever. Further in 6:7-8, *the actual vessels of the
> earthly temple* are committed to the earth to be preserved
> for future use in the restored Jerusalem.

Within the framework of 2B, the passage in question refers to the First
Temple. 4:2-7 says, therefore, that the First Temple was not what God
had in mind when he spoke the words of Isa 49:16. I would agree with
Charles that this is a denigration of the First Temple, and *a fortiori* of the
Second Temple as well, for our author apparently shared the view that the
Second Temple could not compare to the First (2B 68:6-7). I cannot agree
with Charles that this makes this passage inconsistent with 2B 6:9. Our
author intends to relativize the importance of any earthly Temple at all,
but he does not find this to be in contradiction with the rebuilding of the
Temple in the sixth century, B.C.E. The following paragraphs look at 2B
4:2-7 more closely.

We first look at the quotation from Isaiah 49:16 in 2B 4:2. It is likely
that the author knew the context of this verse and expected his readers to
know it as well. It is taken from Second Isaiah, a book written for the
Jewish exiles during the destruction of the First Temple. In other words,
it is taken from a book which does refer to the event which the author is
allegedly describing. The verse in its original context promises a rebuilding of the ruined city of Jerusalem and assures that God will never forget
Zion (49:15). Given that context, the author makes an astounding assertion. That verse did not apply to "this building now built in your midst" at
all! Rather, it applied to the building which is "preserved" (*nṭr*) with God,
and this building is presumably in heaven with God. The earthly Temple is
not the one God has promised to remember forever. One can only conclude that all similar promises concerning Zion also refer to the heavenly
one and not to the earthly one. If such is the case, then all of Baruch's
questions are answered, because the beliefs upon which they were founded
are accordingly qualified. At the very least, the "forever" of the promises

---

found in the Psalms, in Chronicles, in Ezekiel, and elsewhere are shown to pertain only to the building preserved with God.[22]

2B goes further than other works which criticize the Second Temple, such as 1 En 89:73, T Moses 4:8, and Tobit 14.[23] They deprecate the Second Temple by contrasting it with the first, and/or the one to come. 2B does so by contrasting the earthly Temple with the heavenly. The author's purpose is to take attention away from the earthly Temple *per se* and direct it toward the heavenly sphere.

The author's use of the notion of the heavenly Jerusalem invites close examination. The range of ideas usually discussed under the heading "the heavenly Jerusalem" is wide. However, clear references to a city as such existing in heaven are not terribly frequent.[24] Lohse claims that is is found in rabbinic literature only in some late midrashim.[25] 1 En 90:28ff and 4E 13:36; 7:26 are often referred to as instances of the idea, but a close reading of those passages reveals that they never actually say that the city is in heaven, and, unlike 2B, they see the New Jerusalem as rebuilt on earth.[26] The emphasis in these passages seems to be on the divine origin of a future Temple which will be built in order to replace the Second Temple. It is therefore appropriate that their locus is upon the earth, and not in heaven.

In Rev 21, we see the heavenly Jerusalem only as it descends. The fact of its ending up on earth and its Eden-like characteristics (based upon the similar idea in Ezekiel), as well as the presence of God himself in this city now located on earth, are central to the meaning of the image in Revelation.[27]

---

[22]For example, Ps 125:1-2; 2 Chron 6:2; Ezek 43:9, perhaps Apoc Abr 29.

[23]See also 2B 68:6.

[24]It would be invalid to simply identify the image of the heavenly city with that of the heavenly Temple, or with the heavenly sacred service. The latter is often used to legitimate the seer. This is obviously not the function of the city image, which is used rather to show the divine origin of the future city. 2B's purpose is different as we claim here.

[25]E. Lohse, article on *Sion* in *TDNT*, Vol. VII, p. 326.

[26]G. Stemberger, *Der Leib der Auferstehung*, Rome: Biblical Institute, 1972, pp. 83-84; M. Stone, *Features of the Eschatology of IV Ezra*, unpublished dissertation, Harvard, 1965, pp. 101-103.

[27]C. Rowland, *The Open Heaven*, New York: Crossroad, 1982, p. 429.

It is in Galatians, chapter 4, that we get a closer parallel to 2B 4:3-7. In neither passage is there any idea of the city descending, unlike the passages cited above. In both, there is a comparison between the heavenly Jerusalem and the earthly. In both, the intent of the comparison is the negative statement made about the earthly Jerusalem. In both cases the picture of a Jerusalem located in heaven is a polemical image directed against the earthly city. The author of 2B has brought this image to bear on the presuppositions of the contemporaries of the author in order to negate them. The choice is not, as they may believe, between a flourishing earthly Jerusalem and broken promises. The promises never applied to the earthly Jerusalem in the first place. The author in no way wishes to deny scripture-based hope. However, in relocating the point of application of the promise from the earthly to the heavenly sphere, he has eschewed the literal interpretation of Isaiah.[28]

Nowhere in 2B is it stated that this heavenly Jerusalem will descend to earth. It is not an earthly restoration that Israel should be anticipating. The idea of the heavenly city is not picked up again in the book, as we observed. In the only full description of the oft-mentioned consummation, chapters 49-51, the faithful are gathered together in heaven before God's throne. It is likely, therefore, that the author has made use of an idea current in his time to make a negative point about the earthly Temple.[29] The building of the Second Temple changes nothing, for if the First Temple is not the locus of the fulfilment of God's promises, then certainly the Second Temple is not. The groups for whom the figure of Baruch speaks in chapter 3 are thus answered. For them, the fall of Zion had serious repercussions, because it was the place where God could be reached, that which held the world together, and the center of Israel. 2B makes clear that none of these things are true.

That the real opposition in 2B is between earthly and heavenly, and not between present and future earthly Zion is also supported by a look at the language of this passage, which ties it in with the eschatology of the book

---

[28]The promises of fertility, long life, etc., associated with the messianic age, will be fulfilled on this earth (2B 29; 73-74), but for 2B this is just an interim period, signalling the transition to the other world.

[29]Hebrews uses the heavenly sanctuary idea to make a similar point about the Jewish cult. As far as I know, this is the only instance of the use of the heavenly sanctuary to make a negative point about the physical cult.

as a whole. In the previous chapter of this thesis, I claimed that the author sees the consummation as the total passing away of this world, and the entrance of the righteous into the new world, as portrayed in chapters 49-51. 2B 4:2-7 is thus tied in with this eschatology, and its contrast of the heavenly and earthly serves to make clearer the relation between the destruction of the Temple and the author's view of the consummation. It is not a better Temple or city on earth to which the author looks forward, but rather he anticipates the passing away of everything earthly. In 4E, Rev, and 1 En, the function of the heavenly Temple is to indicate the divine origin of the Temple to be built in the time of fulfilment. Thus the Temple descends in Rev, and is seen on earth in 4E and 1 En. In 2B, on the contrary, the fact that the Temple described in chapter 4 is never said to be on earth confirms our view that its function is to relativize the importance of the earthly Temple.

Paradise is shown to the faithful in chapter 51 afer they have been transformed into glory and have ascended into the abode of the angels, and stand before the divine throne. The connection between the heavenly city and the heavenly Paradise, although it occurs only here, strengthens the author's contrast between the heavenly and earthly realms. In chapters 49-51, Paradise is clearly located in the heavenly realm. This is unusual, for the final consummation, painted in the colors of Eden, takes place on earth as a rule. Jeremias asserts that the site of the future Eden is always on earth except in 2B and 2 En.[30]

The author's method is clear. He does not really develop the notions of the heavenly Jerusalem or the heavenly Paradise as such. He merely employs the ideas and claims that their locus is not earth, but heaven. In so doing, he manages to direct a whole series of hopes associated with them to heaven and away from earth. The placing of these two ideas in proximity here, though it is somewhat awkward, helps in this redirection of hopes.

The use of the same verb (pael of $hw^{>}$) to indicate God's "showing" of Jerusalem and Paradise to Adam, Abraham, and Moses serves to heighten the division being made between earthly and heavenly. Presumably, neither has ever been on earth. At most, certain prominent figures got a

---

[30]J. Jeremias, article on *paradeisos* in *TDNT*, Vol. V, p. 767, n. 18: "Only S. Bar. and Slav. En. put the final consummation in heaven. This is because the two works do not distinguish between the present and the last form of its manifestation." In T Dan 5:12, the New Jerusalem is equated with Eden. 4E 8:52 implies that Eden is on earth in the new age (as is Zion), as does T Dan.

privileged glimpse of it in a revelation. The author makes his point more convincing by citing the specific times as recorded by scripture when these worthies received the revelation: Adam before he sinned, Abraham when he sacrificed, and Moses when he saw the "likeness" of the sanctuary.

God now tells Baruch to do what he has been told to do (4:7). Baruch, however, proposes further objections.

Element II' (5:1)

> And I answered and said: 'So then I am destined to grieve for Zion, for Your enemies will come to this place and pollute Your sanctuary, and lead Your inheritance into captivity, and make themselves masters of those whom You have loved, and they will depart again to the place of their idols, and will boast before them: And what will You do for Your great name?'

God has caused his name to dwell in Jerusalem.[31] Baruch's question implies that the destruction of the Temple will have a negative effect on God's great name. The similarity of this intercession with that of Moses in Num 14 and Exod 32 should be noted. In each case, God's impending action is said to be bad for God himself in some sense, so great was the connection between the survival of the people (and also in this case the survival of Zion) and God's reputation and glory. It is also frequently said that God has called Israel by his name.[32]

Farmer claims that the idea that God had to defend the city and the people for his name's sake motivated the defenders of Jerusalem in the war with the Romans in the first century, C.E.[33] Jeremiah seems to have combatted the same attitude.

---

[31]Dtn 12:5, 11, 21; 14:23; etc.; 2 Chron 6:6; Ps 74:7, 18; 76:1-2; 84:1-2, 7, etc.; often "forever" is stated. R. Abba (article on "Name" in *IDB*, Vol. III, p. 503) states that in Dtn, "name theology" becomes prominent. Before, it was applied to temporary manifestations of Yahweh. "Deuteronomy, however, envisages a permanent manifestation of the divine presence at Jerusalem: there God causes his name to dwell."

[32]Dtn 28:10; 2 Chron 7:14; Isa 43:7; Dan 9:18ff; 2B 21:21.

[33]Farmer bases his case primarily upon the fact that the defenders fight with fanatical perseverence until the sanctuary falls, and then simply give up, in spite of the fact that Josephus says that they could have continued the struggle in the even stronger fortifications of the upper city. Pp. 90ff.

Do not trust in these deceptive words: 'This is the temple of
the Lord, the temple of the Lord, the temple of the Lord.'
(Jer 7:4)

Element III' (5:2-4)

(2) And the Lord said to me: 'My name and My glory are unto
all eternity; and My judgment shall maintain its right in its
own time. (3) And you shall see with your eyes that the enemy
will not overthrow Zion, Nor shall they burn Jerusalem, but
be the ministers of the Judge for the time. (4) But do you go
and do whatsoever I have said unto you.'

Here God's name and glory seem to be more or less equivalent. Indeed,
whereas the deuteronomic school most frequently uses "name" to indicate
the divine presence, Ezekiel and priestly circles more often use "glory."

In 2B 5:2-4, God claims that his name and glory do not depend upon the
survival of the earthly Temple, or upon the physical presence of the
people in the land. His name and his glory are "to all eternity" ($^{c}lm^{\jmath}$
$dl^{c}lm$).

It is difficult to know how to take 5:2c. At first glance it looks as
though it may refer to a future retribution for the enemies. This phrase,
or something quite like it, occurs in two other places in 2B: 48:27 and
85:9. In both cases a general judgment is in view, and one which involves
Baruch's addressees. Given that, and the fact that God immediately begins
to describe the impending attack on Jerusalem as the work of the "ministers of the Judge for the time," we are well advised to take 5:2c as an
insistence that God's judgment be carried out upon Zion. So, far from
adversely affecting God's glory and name, the devastation proves and
confirms his judgeship.

Finally, in 5:5-7, Baruch does what the Lord has ordered him to do in
2:1.

And I went and took Jeremiah, and Adu, and Seriah, and
Jabish, and Gedaliah, and all the honourable men of the
people, and I led them to the valley of Cedron, and I narrated
to them all that had been said to me. And they lifted up their
voice, and they all wept. And we sat there and fasted until
evening.

The intercession has failed. In the original form, the success of the intercession served to confirm the assumptions upon which it was founded. In

this use of the form, the failure of the intercession shows that Baruch's assumptions about the consequences of the destruction of Zion and the dispersion of the people are wrong. God's answers fill this in a bit by contrasting the heavenly with the earthly Temple and city, thereby depreciating the latter, and by denying that God's name and glory are seriously affected by the events which have taken place. Using this literary method, the author has therefore taken issue with current Temple ideology and the Temple piety flowing from it.

Another point to notice is that in the other instances of the form of intercessory bargaining, God always threatens to totally destroy the people. This is not the case in 2B, for God explicitly says that the punishment is "for a time." Nonetheless, Baruch takes the destruction of the city and the exile of the people as an indication of total annihilation of the people. This is precisely the point of his objections in chapter 3, which God refutes in chapter 4. The use of the form itself, therefore, implies a certain view held by Baruch which is later made explicit and subsequently refuted.

The Destruction of Jerusalem (chapters 6-8)

(6:1) And it came to pass on the morrow that, lo! the army of the Chaldees surrounded the city, and at the time of evening, I, Baruch, left the people, and I went forth and stood by the oak. (2) And I was grieving over Zion, and lamenting over the captivity which had come upon the people. (3) And lo! suddenly a strong spirit raised me, and bore me aloft over the wall of Jerusalem. (4) And I beheld, and lo!, four angels standing at the four corners of the city, each of them holding a torch of fire in his hands. (5) And another angel began to descend from heaven, and said unto them: "Hold your lamps, and do not light them till I tell you. (6) For I am first sent to speak a word to the earth, and to place in it what the Lord the Most High has commanded me." (7) And I saw him descend into the Holy of Holies, and take from thence the veil, and the holy ark, and the mercy-seat, and the two tables, and the holy raiment of the priests, and the altar of incense, and the forty-eight precious stones, wherewith the priest was adorned and all the vessels of the tabernacle. (8) And he spoke to the earth with a loud voice: "Earth, earth, earth, hear the word of the Mighty God, and receive what I commit to you, and guard them until the last times, so that when you are ordered, you may restore them, so that strangers may not get possession of them. (9) For the time comes when Jerusalem also will be

delivered for a time, until it is said, that it is again restored
for ever." (10) And the earth opened its mouth and swallowed
them up.

(7:1) And after these things, I heard that angel saying to those
angels who held the lamps: "Destroy, therefore, and overthrow its wall to its foundations, lest the enemy should boast
and say; 'We have overthrown the wall of Zion, and we have
burnt the place of the Mighty God.'" (2) And you have seized
the place where I had been standing before.

(8:1) Now the angels did as he had commanded them, and
when they had broken up the corners of the walls, a voice was
heard from the interior of the Temple, after the wall had
fallen, saying: (2) "Enter, you enemies, and come, you adversaries; for he who kept the house has forsaken it." (3) And I,
Baruch, departed. (4) And it came to pass after these things
that the army of the Chaldees entered and seized the house,
and all that was around it. (5) And they led the people away
captive, and slew some of them, and bound Zedekiah the king,
and sent him to the king of Babylon.

In 6:1-2, Baruch finally does what God had told him to do, and leaves
the people. Again, his mourning is stressed.

In 6:4-8:2 the author combines four traditions to paint a picture of the
destruction of Jerusalem. They are the tradition of the four angels, as
also found in Rev 7:1-3, the tradition of the hiding of the Temple vessels,
as also found in 2 Macc 2, a list of the Temple vessels, and the tradition
which describes the departure from the Temple of God before the
destruction, as preserved also by Josephus and by Tacitus. Our intention
here is to isolate the traditions and to see how the author has adapted
them to his own purposes.

We first examine the tradition of the four angels. In both Rev and 2B,
the story consists of four angels who are about to wreak destruction. They
are halted temporarily by another angel who declares that something else
must be done before the destruction can proceed. Also in common is that
the scene is described by a seer ("I saw") and the fact that the angels are
"standing."

On the other hand, there are also major differences between the ver-
sions found in 2B and in Rev. In Rev, the angels wait to destroy the world;
in 2B, Jerusalem. Rev's angels hold back four winds, whereas in 2B they
carry torches. In Rev the angel who stops the four ascends from the
"rising of the sun," and in 2B he descends from heaven. In Rev the angel

must seal the servants of God before the destruction of the world, whereas in 2B the angel wishes to rescue the sacred vessels from the Holy of Holies. This last point is where we get some interference from the second tradition used by the author.

It has been suggested that in Rev 7:1-3 there is some influence from Ezek 9.[34] There "six men" are to destroy the inhabitants of Jerusalem. A seventh man with a "writing case" is to go through the city, putting a "mark upon the foreheads of the men who sigh and groan over all the abominations that are committed in it." (Ezek 9:4) It has been further suggested that the four destructive winds of Rev can be traced to the four winds in Jer 49:36 which also serve to execute divine wrath.[35] The use of angels as God's agents in retribution is, of course, a commonplace in Jewish and Christian sources.

If the image found in Rev 7:1-3 did indeed result from the combination of the elements listed above, we should inquire whether it was the author of Rev who was the one who brought them together. The following two observations suggest that this is not the case. First, this vision is one of two which interrupts the opening of the seals. It occurs between the sixth and the seventh seals. Further, the author drops the image after using it to introduce the people who are sealed, the 144,000. Second, we have found material in common between 2B 6-8 and Rev 7:1-3. It would seem unlikely that either was directly dependent upon the other. This leaves the probability that both depended upon a common source.

We can observe two ways in which the author had adapted the tradition of the four angels to its present context. In 2B 5:3 the author has God say:

> And you shall see with your eyes that the enemy will not overthrow Zion, nor shall they burn Jerusalem, but be the ministers of the judge for the time.

This corresponds with the purpose given by the angel for the destruction of the city walls by the agents of God, the other angels.

> Destroy, therefore, and overthrow its wall to its foundations, lest the enemy should boast and say: "We have overthrown the wall of Zion, and we have burnt the place of the mighty God."

---

[34] A. Y. Collins, *The Apocalypse*, Wilmington: Michael Glazier, 1979, p. 51.

[35] Ibid.

In chapter 5, it is in response to Baruch's fear of the enemies' boasting that God predicts that the enemies will neither overthrow nor burn Zion. Obviously, the author has found the image of the angels as the destructive agents of God's wrath a congenial one to show that such "boasting" by the enemies is excluded.

Further evidence that the author is adapting the angels tradition to his purposes is found in an inconsistency concerning the role of the torches of the angels. In both 5:3 and 7:1 the point is to prove that the enemies do not burn and overthrow Zion. It is implied then that it is God who does this, since Zion was indeed burned. The angels are furnished with torches to do the burning. Nonetheless, there is no description of the burning in chapter 8. Rather, the angels merely break up the walls of the city. In adding the torches, the author went part way in adapting his source to the present context, but he did not fully adapt it.

This leaves us with the question of why the author would combine the angel tradition with that of the hiding of the vessels. This question is answered by 6:8: "So that strangers may not get possession of them." In other words, this particular tradition, as employed by the author, is a further proof that the enemies have no cause to boast.

This use of the hidden vessels tradition contrasts with its use in 2 Macc 2. There, its context deals with provisions made by Jeremiah for the future restoration of the cult. There is no point made of keeping the vessels out of the hands of the enemies. This function is also that found in the Samaritan use of the hidden vessel traditions.[36] This makes it all the more striking that the author explicitly tells us that his purpose is somewhat different here. The author uses the vessels tradition simply to supplement the angel tradition and to underline God's agency in the destruction of Zion.

2B 6:9 envisages the building of the Second Temple, within the fictional framework of the book. That it is to be restored "for ever" is probably just a matter of translation. The phrase l'lm, as was pointed out before, can mean only "for a long time." Sayler's suggestion that the vessels are to be returned to the heavenly Temple is therefore unnecessary.[37]

The list of "holy vessels" in 6:7 is never picked up anywhere else in the book. Why it is so detailed is unclear. Interestingly enough, the list here

---

[36]M. Collins, "The Hidden Vessels in Samaritan Traditions" *JSJ* 3 (1972) pp. 92-116.

[37]Sayler, "2 Baruch: A Story of Grief and Consolation," SBLASP, Chico: Scholars, 1982, p. 494.

seems closest to that found in Hebrews 9:1ff. In common they have the mention of the Holy of Holies, the veil, the ark, the mercy-seat, the two tables, and the altar of incense. Heb does not include the raiment of the priests with its stones. 2B leaves out the contents of the ark as well as a description of the ark itself, the lampstand, the single table, and the bread of the presence. In addition, both passages refer to the "tent" (*mškn'* in both 2B and the Syriac of Heb; *skēnē* in Greek). There is perhaps a shared tradition here. It may have been included to add a note of authenticity to the author's description.

A final tradition brought in by the author is that which concerns the departure of the divine presence from the Temple before its destruction. It is also found in Josephus and Tacitus.[38] This, of course, follows the pattern of events of the destruction of the First Temple as narrated by Ezekiel 9-11.

The use of this tradition here graphically depicts the absence of God from the Temple, and therefore from the midst of his people. It makes the meaning of the destruction of Jerusalem absolutely clear. The people are no longer to look to Zion for the presence of God in their midst.

We can conclude that in 2B 6-8 the author adapted several traditional pieces in order to make his point graphically that God himself is responsible for the destruction of Zion, and also to make absolutely clear that God has deserted the Temple. This, of course, is the situation which the contemporaries of the author of 2B had to face, and which the book was written to help resolve. Our observations concerning the precise way in which the author used the traditions he had at hand reveal his purpose, and reinforce our interpretation of the message of God in chapters 1-5.

SECTION II (10:1-20:6)

This section begins with a long lament over the destruction of Zion, and ends with God's instruction to Baruch about the covenant.[39] This latter passage turns into a consideration of the necessity of a consummation for all things. In this connection, it is said that it was necessary for Zion to be removed in order that God might "more speedily visit the world in its season." (20:2)[40] This puts the reflections about the fairness of God's ways

---

[38]Josephus, War VI 300; Tacitus, The Histories, 5:13.

[39]See the analysis of this section in chapter two of this thesis.

[40]This is the only occurrence of "visit" (*s‘r*) in 2B. Charles takes this as visit "in a bad sense." *APOT*, p. 492.

which are found in this section (especially 14:3-19) firmly in the context of the destruction of Zion.

The section moves from a profound attitude of lament on Baruch's part to God's explaining the necessity of the passing of Zion. The section as a whole, then, has as its basic thrust the correction of Baruch's attitude. This must be kept in mind as we analyze the lament itself.

Although we have in the preceding paragraph employed the usual designation of chapters 10-12, i.e., "lament," this appellation needs to be questioned. It is true that Baruch himself calls his words a "lament." "I lamented (^{5}lyt) with the following lamentation ($^{5}wlyt^{5}$) over Zion." (10:5) Nonetheless, when one compares the form of what we have in chapters 10-12 with the laments found in the psalter, the difference is striking.[41] The laments in the psalter are made up of three major parts into which other elements can then be worked: (1) opening invocation and appeal to God for help; (2a) description of distress; (2b) request for help; (3) expression of confidence in God's aid.[42] In general, then, the lament is addressed to God.

In 2B 10-12, element 1 is missing entirely. There is no direct invocation of God. The description of the distress (element 2a) is present only very indirectly. What little description there is of the devastation of Zion is subordinated to the direct address to the various groups (10:7b-c; 10:10b, 12d, 16c-d; 11:2 etc.). Element 2b, the request for aid, is also absent. 11:3c, "O Lord, how have You borne (it)," hardly qualifies. It is more of a cry of indignation that God would allow such a thing to happen. Chapter 12 is a threat to the enemies, but is still not formally a direct request to God. Neither does this chapter (12) have the characteristics of the expression of confidence (element 3) which we would expect in a lament. In form, it is not far from the kind of conclusion found in Ps 6, which is a lament.[43] Ps 6:8-9 is in the form of a direct address to the enemies. Nonetheless, the command to the enemies to withdraw is based in verse 9 on the confidence of the author of the psalm that God will hear his prayer, a motif which is not present in 2B 12. Furthermore, the actual prediction of the downfall of the enemies in Ps 6:10 is in the third person.

The Book of Lamentations seems to be an expansion of and a modifica-

---

[41]See Harnisch's instructive analysis of the *Volksklagelieder* in 4E (pp. 20ff). Also, see Brandenburger's correction of Harnisch with regard to the *Eingangsklage* of 4E 9:29-37 in *Die Verborgenheit Gottes im Weltgeschehen*, Zurich: Theologischer Verlag Zurich, 1981, pp. 65ff.

[42]R. Murphy, "Psalms," *JBC*, p. 572.

[43]Murphy, p. 572.

tion of the lament form. All of the elements are present. The description of the distress is greatly expanded, the invocation and request are placed at the end (chapter 5), and the expression of confidence comes before the invocation and request for aid (4:21-22). Therefore, this work also fails to provide us with a good formal model for the creation in 2B 10-12.

In form, 2B 10-12 is a reversal of such psalms as Ps 148 and the Song of the Three Young Men.[44] They are hymns of praise in which all of creation, including mankind, is directly invited to praise God. In 2B 10-12, all of creation, including mankind, is told to stop its natural functions and to mourn. A comparison of the order in which parts of the world are addressed in 2B 10 and the Song of the Three Young Men indicates that there may even be a common dependence upon a list.

2B 10	*Song*
v 8 Sirens of sea Lilin from desert Shedim and dragons from forest	vv 57-59 whales and creatures of the sea birds beasts and cattle
vv 9-10 earth giving fruits vine offering wine	vv 52-54 earth mountains and hills all that grows on the earth

vv 11-12
heavens with dew and
  rain
	vv 36, 40, 42, 46, 48
	heavens, sun and moon, rain
	  and dew, dew and snows,
	  light and darkness

vv 13-16 mankind	v 60 mankind
v 18 priests	v 62 priests

---

[44]Bogaert devotes an entire chapter to what would appear to be our topic: "Les lamentations sur la chute du Temple" (Volume I, pp. 127-176). In fact, he connects the various "lamentations" only by means of their common subject matter. His comparison is not of literary forms, but has to do with the established practices of mourning over the ruined Temple.

Murphy reminds us that von Rad demonstrated that psalms such as Ps 148 and the Song of the Three Young Men show the influence of *Listenwissenschaft*. This would explain the closeness of the kinds of things mentioned in both poems. It does not, however, explain the way in which 2B reverses the Song. In the context of deliverance from danger, the Song invites all of nature and humankind to share in the praise and thanksgiving due to God. In 2B, because there has been no deliverance, and the Temple has been delivered up, the author points out the impossibility of praise (which for him takes place in the cult—10:10b-c, 12d, 16c-d), and invites all of nature and humankind to join him in mourning. Keeping in mind the fact that this section in its content and in its very structure corrects this lament of Baruch, we can see that this belief that praise for God is now cut off and mourning is proper for all creation is refuted by the author.

The destruction of the Temple, with the concomitant cessation of the cult, should, in Baruch's view, result in the stoppage of the fruitfulness of the earth. Baruch represents that part of the Temple ideology which sees the natural processes of the world, as well as the fertility of the land, as being dependent upon the proper functioning of the Temple and cult.

2B 10:13-16, in which Baruch tells the human race to stop reproducing, recalls the question of Baruch in 3:8. "And shall the multitude of souls be taken away, and the nature of man not again be named?" Baruch has not yet been persuaded that his attitude toward the destruction of Zion is wrong. The element of correction is important. Baruch must still change his views.

That Baruch retains his outlook which underlay the questions of chapter 3 and of 5:1 is also proved by his insistent "death wish"[45] found at the beginning of his words (10:6-7) and between his lament and the *Drohwort*[46] of chapter 12. (11:4-7)

The attitude of acute mourning conveyed especially by 2B 10:9-10 recalls the viewpoint of those people encountered by R. Joshua in Baba Bathra 60b.[47]

> Our Rabbis taught: When the Temple was destroyed for the second time, large numbers in Israel became ascetics, binding themselves neither to eat meat nor to drink wine. R. Joshua got into conversation with them and said to them: My sons, why do you not eat meat nor drink wine? They replied: Shall

---

[45]This is Sayler's phrase. See *Promises,* pp. 14-38.
[46]Harnisch, p. 77.
[47]J. Neusner, *Development,* p. 114.

we eat flesh which used to be brought as an offering on the
altar, now that this altar is in abeyance? Shall we drink wine
which used to be poured as a libation on the altar, but now no
longer? He said to them: If that is so, we should not eat bread
either, because the meal offerings have ceased. They said:
(That is so, and) we can manage with fruit. We should not eat
fruit either, (he said), because there is no longer an offering
of firstfruits. Then we can manage with other fruits (they
said). But, (he said), we should not drink water, because there
is no longer any ceremony of the pouring of water. To this
they could find no answer, so he said to them: My sons, come
and listen to me. Not to mourn at all is impossible, because
the blow has fallen. To mourn overmuch is also impossible,
because we do not impose on the community a hardship which
the majority cannot endure . . .

There follows the famous rule of leaving a little of one wall bare when
one stuccos one's house, etc. This form of mourning is allowed and
recommended.

For so it says, "If I forget thee, O Jerusalem, let my right
hand forget, let my tongue cleave to the roof of my mouth if
I remember thee not, if I prefer not Jerusalem above my
chief joy." (Ps 137:5-6)[48]

In 2B 10, Baruch tells the vines not to bear and the earth not to bring
forth fruit. In Baba Bathra 60b the mourners refuse to eat meat, or to
drink the fruit of the vine. In both cases, the reason given for the proposed action is that sacrifices are no longer offered upon the altar. The
opponents of R. Joshua and the holders of the attitude represented by
Baruch's lament have much in common. Much in the manner in which Paul
picks up the slogans and axioms of his opponents in Corinth, R. Joshua
undoubtedly defended his views on the basis of the same scriptural verses

---

[48]Note our previous discussion about the necessity of including R.
Joshua among the mourners for Zion, because of his opposition to
rebuilding the Temple by means of warfare, and our drawing of a parallel
between Baruch and R. Joshua. Note also the fact that Baruch represents
a group mourning over the destruction of Zion, and that it is part of the
purpose of the author to correct what he sees to be an unreasonable
amount of mourning. We have already pointed out that a viewpoint such as
that contained in Ps 137 is that of the opponents. Here we see R. Joshua
using the same citation.

as did his antagonists. This method will become important in our discussion below of Baruch's speech in section III. Thus, Joshua (and Baruch) insists that he does indeed remember Zion, but in a way more consistent with common sense and the will of God.

10:18-19 allows the author to extend his invitation to mourn to the Temple personnel, just as the Song of the Three Young Men had invited them to praise God. Verse 17 breaks the pattern of the list. It does not really belong to the address to mankind of 10:13-16, for those verses are concerned with procreation of the race. The opening of v 18 seems a new beginning: *ʾntwn dyn khnʾ*. The author has broken into his own use of the reversal of the hymn of praise with this material in v 17 in order to characterize the attitude of Baruch in a general fashion. Baruch feels that there is no longer anything beautiful or gracious within the grasp of humanity. A consideration of the use of the words beauty (*swprʾ*) and gracefulness (*yʾywtʾ*) in the remainder of the book indicates how God corrects Baruch with respect to this judgment.

The two words in question occur together several times in the book. The most important occurrence is 51:10. In chapter 10, Baruch gives up all thought of beauty and loveliness. In 51:10, God points out that he need not give up hope of these qualities, but he should look for them in the future world, and not here. In 82:7 and 83:12, beauty and gracefulness characterize the enemies in this age, but is limited to this age for them.

2B 51:3 also places the loveliness (*yʾywtʾ*) of the righteous in the future world. In 21:23 and 54:8, it is a quality of God, the revelation of which the author longs for. In 51:11, beauty (*šwprʾ*) belongs to the world of glory.

The author also adds 11:1-2, bringing into consideration the problem caused by the prosperity of the enemies, and the contrasting desolation of Zion. This is a problem which is at the forefront of concern in 4E, so it is in the air at the time of writing of 2B. As shown in the previous chapter, the author deals with this problem by investigating the true nature of prosperity in this section and the next. Again, Baruch's attitude of despair over this situation is proved to be rooted in a false understanding of the nature of the two worlds.

Section II begins with a lament over the destruction of Jerusalem and a cry for vengeance by Baruch. It ends in chapter 20 with an assertion by God that Zion indeed had to be removed, to make way for the consummation.

SECTION III (21:1-34:1)

For our purposes in this chapter, the most important part of this section is the speech at the end, 31:3-32:7.

(31:3) Hear, O Israel, and I will speak to you, and give ear, O seed of Jacob, and I will instruct you. (4) Forget not Zion, but hold in remembrance the anguish of Jerusalem. (5) For lo! the days come, when everything that is shall become the prey of corruption and be as though it had not been.

(32:1) But as for you, if you prepare your hearts, so as to sow in them the fruits of the law, it shall protect you in that time in which the Mighty One is to shake the whole creation. (2) Because after a little time the building of Zion will be shaken in order that it may be built again. (3) But that building will not remain, but will after a time be rooted out, and will remain desolate until the time. (4) And afterwards it must be renewed in glory, and perfected for evermore. (5) Therefore we should not be distressed so much over the evil which has now come as over that which is still to be. (6) For there will be a greater trial than these two tribulations when the Mighty one will renew his creation. (7) And now do not draw near to me for a few days, nor seek me till I come to you.

The structure of 31:3-32:7 is basically the same as that of Baruch's testament in 44:5-45:2, in section IV.

Speech of Section III	*Speech of Section IV*

Forget not Zion
but hold in remembrance the
    anguish of Jerusalem
    (31:4)
	See what has befallen Zion
	and what has happened to
	    Jerusalem (44:5)

For the days come when
    everything that is shall
    become the prey of cor-
    ruption . . . (31:5)
	For the judgment of the Mighty
	    One shall thereby be made
	    known . . . (44:6)

If you prepare your hearts
    . . . it shall protect
    you . . . (32:1)
	If you endure and persevere . . .
	    the times will change over you
	    . . . (44:7)

Because (then a description of the future) (32:2-4)	*Because* (then a description of the future) (44:8-15)
Therefore, we should not be distressed (32:5)	*Therefore*, so far as you are able, instruct the people (45:1)
For there will be a greater trial (32:6)	*For* if you teach them, you will quicken them (45:2)

Both speeches are followed by objections of the people to which Baruch responds. The speech in chapters 44-45 is preceded by Baruch's announcement of his impending departure from this life (as part of the testament form) (44:2) and then by a command to the elders who must teach people (44:3). This makes the speech fit its context, and creates some lack of symmetry between the two speeches.

In spite of this difference, the two speeches are very alike. In view of the importance of the speeches in the book, we should not be surprised to discover this careful structuring by the author. Further, we should take the careful structuring as a signal to regard these speeches as particularly helpful in interpreting the book as a whole.

The form of each of the speeches compared above is remarkably like that of Mark 13 as analyzed by Gaston. Gaston claims that the basic thread of Mark 13 consists of what he calls "eschatological paraclesis."[49] There is a series of commands, each grounded in instruction about what the future holds. A good example is Mk 13:9.

> But take heed to yourselves, *FOR* they will deliver you up to councils; and you will be beaten in synagogues . . .

2B 31:4 is a command, followed by 31:5 which is an instruction about the future. 31:5 is introduced by "for" (*gyr*). Thus, formally 31:4-5 corresponds to the basic unit of "eschatological paraclesis."

32:1 is the equivalent of a command, rooted in the language and mode of expression of the covenant (as will be discussed in the next chapter), and is followed in 32:3-4 by a description of future events introduced by "because" (*mtwl*).

32:5 is also an indirect command, expressed in the form of "it is necessary for us to . . ." (*mtbᶜyꜣ ln d*). This is followed by 32:6 which again is a description of future events, introduced by "for" (*gyr*).

---

[49]L. Gaston, *No Stone on Another*, Leiden: Brill, 1970, p. 15.

A key question for us is precisely what is meant by the command to remember Zion. If indeed the intent of the author is to distract the attention of his readers away from the destruction, how does this command fit? This question is sharpened when one examines the command in 32:5, which supports our interpretation of the intent of the author. 32:5 is an exhortation *not* to be distressed over what has happened.

This brings us back to our suggestion that just as Paul picked up the slogans of his opponents at Corinth, and as R. Joshua used the very same scripture as his adversaries when refuting them, so also our author puts into the mouth of Baruch a phrase being used by the people whom he wished to correct. They were probably urging their fellows to "remember Zion." Our author says, "Yes, indeed, remember Zion, but in the correct way and for the right reasons." What is the correct way? From our passage one can draw the conclusion that distress is inappropriate. If not distress, then what? 31:5 supposedly supplies the ground for the command to remember Zion.[50] It is that "everything that is shall become the prey of corruption."

In the previous chapter, we demonstrated that the author takes great pains to describe the two aeons. The future aeon is equivalent to heaven, and the entrance of the righteous into it is laid out in chapters 49-51.

In 31:4-5 we see the author applying his view of the two worlds to Zion. Zion has become an example of the transitoriness of the world. This accords well with the view of the fall of Zion espoused in chapter 20. The author has answered his opponents using their own terminology: "Yes, remember Zion, but as an example of how all must inevitably pass away so that the righteous may truly enter the permanent presence of God."

32:2-4 points the audience away from the destructions of the First and Second Temple and towards a final renewal of the Temple and of creation. Does the author anticipate the restoration of the earthly Temple? Given the world view which the author elaborates in this very section, it is hard to imagine such a phrase as "perfected for evermore" (32:4) meaning anything less than the passing away of this world. How is there room in the eschatology we saw in the previous chapter for a renewed Temple?

The phrase "renewal of creation" (32:6) fits most easily into the eschatology of Isaiah. The renewal of the "building of Zion" also fits that image (Isa 62:6-9). The contradiction between 2B 32:1-7 and the eschatology outlined in the previous chapter must therefore be acknowledged. Here we

---

[50]See Gaston, p. 15. Our conclusion here is based on his remarks concerning the nature of the form "eschatological paraclesis."

have the earlier eschatology apparently unaltered by the author's reflections upon the natures of the two worlds. That this occurs in the speech
concluding section III is especially intriguing, since this section begins
with the prayer (chapter 21) which contains some of the author's clearest
reflections on the natures of the two worlds. Thus in section III the tension between the two sets of eschatological language mentioned in the
previous chapter of this thesis is present.

It would appear that our author did not wish to replace the eschatology
of the tradition of Isaiah wholesale. Rather, he is trying to bolster the
hope of the people in the future. In so doing he can still refer to a
renewed Zion. Nonetheless he tempers this with his own novel solution to
the problem of the distress of the present time. We may then read all of
section III, which is full of traditional apocalyptic units concerning the
arrival of the eschaton, in the light of the prayer in chapter 21. 2B thus
represents a transitional stage in which we find statements from two
different kinds of eschatologies. In this context the "renewal of creation"
could refer to the passing away of earth and the entrance of the righteous
into heaven. In that connection, it may be significant that the author did
not choose the terminology of the renewal of heaven and earth.

Sections II and III contain reflections about the contrasting nature of
the two aeons which are unique in what is normally considered apocalyptic
literature. Here in the end of section III, in the address of Baruch to the
elders, those reflections bear fruit when they are applied to Zion. One is
to keep firmly in mind that all is passing away. Therefore, one should not
remember Zion with distress, but only as a reminder about the natures of
the two worlds.

SECTION IV (35:1-47:1)

This section begins with Baruch's second lamentation over the destruction of Zion (chapter 35). We have already analyzed the structure of the
closing speech (ch 44) of this section in our discussion of the speech in
chapters 31-32. It is in the form of a testament. Von Nordheim has shown
that in this genre it is the *Verhaltenserweisung* which predominates.[51] All
sorts of material can be introduced into the testament form in order to
support and motivate the reader to carry out that to which the author
exhorts him or her.

In chapter 44, Baruch's testamentary speech begins and ends with the

---

[51] E. von Nordheim, *Die Lehre der Alten*, Leiden: Brill, 1980, p. 242.

exhortation to the elders and a few others to admonish the people and to teach them the Law. In 44:5 there is a command to look at Zion and its anguish. Every other element in this speech is subordinated to these commands, being introduced by "for" or "because." This confirms the thesis of von Nordheim, and causes us to look particularly at the commands themselves to discern the author's purpose. The speech can be schematized as follows.

> Do not withdraw from the Law. Admonish the people (3)
>> FOR God is no respecter of persons. (4)
> See what happened to Zion. (5)
>> FOR God's judgment is visible there. (6)
>> FOR if you obey the Law,
>> you will see the consolation of Zion. (7)
>
> BECAUSE "whatever is now is nothing, but that which
> shall be is very great."
>> FOR the corruptible world will pass away (9-10)
>> FOR the future world will not pass away (11-12)
>> FOR the Law-abiders will inherit the future world (13-14)
>> FOR the Law-abiders will be rewarded and the sinners
>> punished (15)
>
> THEREFORE instruct the people (45:1)
>> FOR thereby you will give them life (2)

In 44:5 the destruction of Zion is an example of God's relentless justice, and therefore of the fact that he is no respecter of persons. This is demonstrated by the reason given to remember Zion, as found in 44:6. Remember Zion, "for the judgment of the Mighty One is (thereby) made known." This agrees with the view of the destruction at the beginning of 2B (chapter 1), and is an instance of the third solution of the author to the problem of the destruction as stated at the beginning of this chapter, viz., the destruction as punishment for sin.

44:7 also mentions Zion. It stands out in this speech, because it is a form used frequently by our author. It is a conditional sentence, in which the protasis consists of obedience to the Law, and the apodosis promises future reward. In this case, the future reward is the "consolation of Zion." Thus, it is a reversal of the anguish of 44:5. But what does the author mean by the "consolation of Zion?"

We are aided in answering this last question by noticing that 44:7 is immediately followed by a lengthy section contrasting the two worlds in an ontological way. The first part of the speech (44:3-7) had concentrated upon obedience to the Law as the way to salvation, with Zion used as an illustration of God's impartiality. The second part (44:8-15) deals with the two-world schema. Formally, it is seen as a reason for the first part of the speech. *mtl d* indicates a break with the series of *gyr's* which has gone before, and so begins a new part of the speech, yet a part which supplies the reason for what has gone before. The author adduces the two-world concept as an incentive to obey the Law. Verses 13-14 make the connection even clearer.

> For these are they who shall inherit that time which has been spoken of, and theirs is the inheritance of the promised time. These are they who have acquired for themselves treasures of wisdom, and with them are found stores of understanding, and from mercy have they not withdrawn, and the truth of the law they have preserved.

It is evident that 44:7 is pivotal in the speech. Its protasis points back to the exhortation to obey the Law (which is motivated by God's impartiality which in turn is illustrated by the destruction of Zion), and its apodosis points to the future reward, which is put in terms of the reversal of the pain of Zion, but is explained in great detail by the long passage which follows in 44:8-15. Given this context of and function of 44:7, one can see, *pace* Charles,[52] that it is hardly a case of an expectation of a future rebuilding of Zion in this world that is contained in 44:7. It is in the middle of a speech entirely devoted to an exposition of the passing of all which is part of this world. We have seen, and will see again, that this world includes the earthly Temple. By placing this verse in this context, the author reinterprets the hope for the consolation of Zion. It now must mean the rewarding of those Jews faithful to the Law by giving them eternal life in the new world.

The inclusion of forgetfulness of the present time in the description of the future (44:9) underlines this point. One remembers Zion for a specific purpose, in this case to remind oneself of the impartiality of God's justice.

---

[52] *APOT*, p. 503. Harnisch feels that the author is simply taking over traditional material here without rewriting it to express his own point of view (p. 212, n. 2). I think that he is taking over a slogan of his opponents, deliberately not altering it in order to use his opponents' language against them by putting it in another context.

One does not remember Zion in order to dwell on the catastrophe, or to nurse hopes of a rebuilt city.

This use of the destruction in connection with God's impartiality is also apparent in chapter 13.

> You who have drunk the strained wine, drink you also of its dregs, the judgment of the Lofty One who has no respect of persons. On this account he had aforetime no mercy on His own sons, but afflicted them as enemies because they sinned.

SECTION V (47:1-52:7)

The Temple and Zion are not explicitly mentioned in this section. This in itself is significant, since the section contains the fullest description of the fate of the righteous. This takes place especially in chapters 49-51, and has been examined at length in the previous chapter of this thesis. We have already mentioned that the occurrence of Paradise in chapter 51 forms a link between this chapter and chapter 4. This leads us to recall that in chapters 3-5 the main problem which is confronted by Baruch is the loss of God's presence in the Temple. This is dramatically portrayed in 8:2. Now, in chapter 51, the righteous finally re-enter God's presence, symbolized by the throne and the ministering angels. This is another way of saying what the author has already said in chapter 4: God's real presence is in heaven. It is there where our hopes should be placed. In chapter 4, the author picked up an idea current in his time, without really developing it. In these chapters, we must be closer to the author's own thinking. Although he did not make up his description in 49-51 out of whole cloth, his hand is evident in the connected flow of this passage.

SECTION VI (53:1-77:17)

The bulk of this section is taken up by a review of history. Its sweep includes what amounts to creation (God sends forth the great cloud) and moves to the Messianic Age, which is only an interim period before the final consummation.

Anitra Kolenkow has analyzed this section of 2B in detail in her dissertation. In the next chapter we will attempt to relate it to the covenant in 2B. Our present interest is in what it has to tell us about the attitude of the author to the Temple.

Kolenkow points out that the closest parallels we have to 2B's review of history can be found in the ten-week apocalypse of 1 En, and in the Life of Adam and Eve 29. The chart below depends upon her analysis.[53]

2B 56-74	1 En 93, 91	Vita 29
(1) Adam		
	(1) Enoch	
	(2) Deceit, Noah	
(2) Abraham	(3) Abraham	
(3) Evil-doers in Egypt		
(4) Moses, Law	(4) Visions, Law	Lord appears, Law
(5) Evil of Amorites		
(6) Temple built	(5) Temple built	Temple built
(7) Jeroboam		
(8) Hezekiah		
(9) Manasseh		
(10) Josiah		
(11) Zion destroyed Dispersion	(6) Temple burned, Dispersion	Temple burned Dispersion
	(7) Apostates and elect	
(12) Second Temple Evils Bliss	(8) Second Temple (9) Evil judged (10) Judgment, Righteousness	Second Temple Evils Righteousness

I would agree with Kolenkow that there is a shared order which in the cases of 2B and 1 En extends from Abraham to the final bliss, and which extends in all three from the giving of the Law to the final happy situation of the righteous.

The periodization of history in 2B differs from these two and from any others of my acquaintance in that there is a rigorous pattern of alternating good and evil periods. There is some alternation visible in 1 En, but it is not carried through schematically. For example, both apostates and elect receive attention in the seventh week. In Vita 29, there is no explicit periodization of history *per se*. This rigorous pattern is probably the work of our author.

---

[53]The numbers in parentheses refer to the waters in 2B and the weeks in 1 En.

This last statement is confirmed by chapter 69, where the twelve periods of the interpreted vision correspond to six "courses" (*dwbr*) of evil and six of good works.[54] This explanation by the author gives us the key to his purpose. Although he remains well within the apocalyptic fold by insisting that it is God who has crafted history according to this deliberate pattern, 69:3ff makes plain that the goodness or badness of each period depends totally and entirely upon the good or evil works of the people living within it. This is carried out strictly within the actual descriptions of the periods.

A good point of comparison to illustrate the point is the period of the building of the Temple. 1 En 93:7 states baldly:

> And after that in the fifth week, at its close, the house of glory and dominion shall be built for ever.

2B 61:7 looks quite different.

> And the judgment of the rulers was then seen to be without guilt, and the righteousness of the precepts of the Mighty One was accomplished with truth. And the land (which) was then beloved by the Lord, and *because its inhabitants sinned not,* it was glorified beyond all lands, and the city Zion ruled then over all lands and regions.

A causal connection is drawn between the prosperity of Zion and the righteousness of its inhabitants (*mtl dl' ḥtyn hww ʿmwryh*).

Because of the above observations, I am in agreement with Kolenkow when she claims that the author of 2B has "turned the structures of apocalyptic literature to the services of parenesis."[55] In this case, the parenesis is a general one. This is demonstrated by the very general nature of the sins at the center of the evil periods inserted between Abraham and Moses, and again between Moses and David. The author is not so much interested in specific sins as he is in drawing the comprehensive connection between the behavior of people and the character of their period.

---

[54]Kolenkow's problem of the lack of specific vices or virtues for each of the periods results from her sticking to Charles' translation for *dwbr*. The problem is removed when one merely takes its meaning as "course" or period of time. See Harnisch, p. 263.

[55]Kolenkow, p. 144ff.

In the prayer of Baruch which occurs between the vision of section VI and its interpretation, the author stresses personal responsibility, and proclaims as just the punishment of those who do not obey the Law. The address concluding the section (chapter 77) is a call to rededicate the people to the covenant, a call which they accept in 77:11. Given that framework, it is not surprising that the interpretation of the vision concentrates upon the link between actions and their consequences.

We have already remarked upon the causal connection between the behavior of the people and the prosperity of Zion in the time of David and Solomon. This is the first historically justified spot at which the author could have introduced the topic of Zion. Between the period of David and that of the fictional present of the author, i.e., the first destruction of the Temple, he has inserted four periods into the scheme as it is shared by 2B and 1 En. These are the bad period of Jeroboam, the good one of Hezekiah, the evil one of Manasseh, and the good one of Josiah. Again, the author retains his pattern alternating good and evil periods. Of particular interest to us is that he has chosen four kings of the Jews whose actions had specific repercussions for the cult.

Jeroboam's iniquity had severe consequences on the fertility of the land and eventually led to the exile of the northern kingdom. Hezekiah's reliance upon his righteousness and good works saved the city from destruction. Manasseh's impiety caused the "praise of the Most High" to be removed from the sanctuary. Josiah's restoration of the purity of the cult had as its consequence an eternal reward for him.

The moral to be drawn from all of this is that the welfare of the city, and of the people within the land, depends upon the actions of human beings. This is in spite of the fact that God fashions the whole of history. The stories of the four kings should be read with chapter 1 of 2B in mind.

> For the former tribes were forced by their kings to commit
> sin, but these two of themselves have been forcing and com-
> pelling their kings to commit sin. (1:3)

God goes on to deliver the sentence upon the people for such sinfulness. In the present, the people as a whole are sinners, and this results in the destruction of Zion. In the past, the behavior of the kings led to the prosperity or the destruction of Zion. In any case, Zion's fate depends upon its inhabitants.

Chapter 67, which deals with the fictional present of the author, adds weight to our interpretation. In that chapter the point is forcefully made that Zion's fate depends not upon herself, but rather is related to God's judgment of the people. Especially important in the understanding of this passage is the very verse which Charles sees as intrusive, 67:4.[56]

> But how will it serve towards his righteous judgment?

It should be noted that this verse is in the form of a question. As such, it belongs to the series of questions in 67:2-4, paraphrased below.

> Do you think that the angels rejoice over the destruction of Zion?
> Do you think that God is happy, or that his name is glorified because of it?
> But how does it serve his judgment, which is just?

That 67:4 is the culmination of this series of questions is underlined by the fact that 67:5 indicates a clear break with the series: "But after these things shall the dispersed . . ." It is evident that 67:4, like the two preceding questions, refers directly to the destruction of Jerusalem in Baruch's time. The first two questions are rhetorical, and seem meant to point out to a certain group of mourners the logical consequence of their attitude. By mourning over the destruction of Jerusalem, and exhibiting an attitude such as that embodied in the laments of chapters 10-12 and 35, they ignore the motive behind God's action, and therefore imply that it is capricious. He does it simply for his own pleasure. The questions put the mourners on the spot and force them to recognize the full implications of their outlook.

Having pointed out that those who mourn over Zion in an unreflective way accuse God and his angels of caprice, the author goes on in 67:4 to challenge them to ask the truly relevant question. What does the destruction imply with respect to God's judgment? This is a challenge for them to give the obvious answer which the reader has had since chapter one, and which Baruch utters in his prayer at the beginning of this section in chapter 54. It is the answer which will cause them to acknowledge their own guilt and to rededicate themselves to the covenant as the appropriate response to the destruction.

67:5-8 make clear the impiety which will be worldwide following the destruction of Zion. It is an adaptation of the theme of the multiplication of evil before the end.

In chapter 68 we encounter the more traditional form of the depreciation of the Second Temple.

---

[56] APOT, p. 516.

> And at that time after a little interval Zion will again be
> builded, and its offerings will again be restored, and the
> priests will return to their ministry, and also the Gentiles will
> come to glorify it. Nevertheless, not fully as in the beginning.

The negative attitude toward the Temple is characterized as being based
upon its inadequacy in comparison with the First Temple in 1 En 89:73, T
Moses 4:8; Tobit 14. This element is present in our passage. This is not the
point of our author's use of the tradition, however. Were this the case, the
author would not have included the statement about the Gentiles glorify-
ing the Second Temple. This element is taken from the tradition that in
the final golden age the Temple will be the focus of worship for the entire
world (Isa 2:2-4; 49:22-23; 56:6-8; 60:1-3). His use of this motif may be
due to his desire to locate many of the promises associated with the
Temple and the Messianic Age in this world. In putting this period in the
past (from the point of view of the reader) the author subtly indicates
that one should not look for the glorification of the earthly Temple as
part of the golden age any longer. This is not to be the object of hope.

Throughout most of 2B, the author has clearly kept to his fiction about
the time of Baruch. We have already indicated in our discussion of the
first section of 2B that if the author denigrates the First Temple, then
this applies *a fortiori* to the second. In chapter 68 the author himself
makes the same point explicitly. If one agrees that he relativizes the loss
of the First Temple in his work, then this passage is his way of making the
same point with respect to the second.

We now leave the review of history to investigate Baruch's reaction to
it in chapter 75.[57] The conditional sentence in v 7 implies that if one has
the correct view of history, one will "rejoice regarding that which has
been." The great fact of the past in 2B's estimation is the fall of the
Temple. This forms the ever-present backdrop to the book. Thus, we are
justified in seeing that referred to here (as in chapter 43, for example).
That destruction is not cause for mourning, but for joy, if one views the
history of Israel from a covenantal framework, alluded to in the phrase
"He who brought us out of Egypt," repeated in vv 7 and 8.

---

[57] For a general discussion of the functions of periodizations of history,
see L. Hartman, "The Functions of Some So-called Apocalyptic Timetables," *NTS* 22 (1976), pp. 1-14. For the "apocalyptic" use of history
versus the "rabbinic" one, see Rössler, *Gesetz und Geschichte*, Neukirchen, Neukirchener Verlag, 1960.

SECTION VII (77:18-87:1)

Since the epistle is a kind of summary of 2B 1-77, we expect to find the author's major points about Zion recapitulated there. Such is indeed the case. In 79:2, Baruch writes that Zion was destroyed because of the sins of Israel. In 80:1-4, God's agency in the destruction is stressed in the same terms as those used in section I. In 83:4, the recipients of the letter are urged not to be distressed over the loss of Zion. 85:4 places Zion clearly in this corruptible aeon, and so relativizes its loss.

CONCLUSIONS

The author of 2B wanted to direct the attention of Israel away from the destruction of the Temple and Zion as a cause for mourning towards the real place of God's presence, heaven. He was writing a kind of revisionist theology--one which reassessed the place of the city of Jerusalem and its Temple in Judaism. It was a theology based upon a world-view which saw the present world as inherently transitory and therefore inferior to the other, eternal world now existing with God.

This new view placed the Temple of Jerusalem squarely in this passing world. Its destruction was therefore not only unworthy of despair, but was even a necessary step towards the passing of a world which of its nature must pass. The true center of Judaism could not be this Temple. Rather, the author saw the necessity of depicting the religion's heavenly goal and the Law as the means to attain it. Such a depiction radically alters the Jewish religion as it was known before 70 C.E. Before that date,[58]

> the common religion of the country consisted of three main elements; first, the Hebrew scriptures, second, the Temple, and third, the common and accepted practices of the ordinary folk--their calendar, their mode of living, their everyday practices and rites, based on these first two.

Second Baruch redefines Judaism in view of the disappearance of its cultic center. This effort is analogous to the efforts made at Qumran to redefine the Temple once it had been lost to them.[59] Unlike Qumran,

---

[58] J. Neusner, "Formation," p. 21.

[59] B. Gärtner, *The Temple and the Community in Qumran and the New Testament*, Cambridge: Cambridge University, 1965. The rabbis followed a similar road in seeing the whole of Israel as the dwelling-place of the Shekinah (Gaston, p. 3).

which saw the community as the new Temple and the fulfilment of the Law as a substitute for atoning sacrifice, 2B relativizes the Temple altogether and sees the Law as a way to move safely from this transitory world to the eternal world of heaven. Its apparent lack of interest in atonement contrasts both with Qumran and with rabbinical views, which introduced a whole series of practices to substitute for sacrificial atonement.[60]

It is perhaps the author's greatest achievement that he gets the people to turn away from the destruction of the Temple precisely by making them look at it in a different light. It becomes for them an example of the corruptibility of this world, and of the inevitability of punishment due to sin. It is no longer the *sine qua non* of contact with the presence of God.

We can now see how the vertical element of the eschatology of the author has served his purpose of trying to come to grips with the loss of Zion. We have also observed how he retains the language of the Isaiah tradition in speaking of a future new creation. To understand what is happening here it is useful to refer to MacRae's treatment of the eschatology of Hebrews.[61]

It has long been recognized that Hebrews contains two different eschatologies. One could be termed traditional apocalyptic (oriented to a future event, and therefore horizontal), and the other a more Alexandrinian approach (influenced by the type of philosophy evident in the middle platonist Philo, and so more vertical). As a solution to the presence of these two eschatologies in Hebrews, MacRae suggests that the author subscribed to the Alexandrinian view, but was writing to a community with a more apocalyptic view. Hebrews was meant to bolster the flagging hope of the addresses by interweaving insights gained from Alexandrinian philosophy with the images and language of apocalyptic. The author did not wish to replace the eschatology of the community to which he wrote, but rather to revitalize it.

I see a similar effort in 2B. Our author can continue to use traditional apocalyptic language, but he interweaves with that language his reflections on the two worlds with which the earlier language is not entirely compatible. Our author perhaps goes further than the author of Hebrews

---

[60]H. Wenschkewitz, *Die Spiritualisierung der Kultusbegriffe*, Leipzig: Eduard Pfeiffer, 1932, pp. 24ff.

[61]G. MacRae, "The Heavenly Temple and Eschatology in the Letter to the Hebrews," *Semeia* 12, Missoula: Scholars, 1978.

in that he seems to wish to change the goal of the people to heaven and to denigrate the hope of an earthly restoration. Even so, he does not totally depart from traditional formulations.

5

The Covenant

SECOND BARUCH AND STECK'S ANALYSIS

O. H. Steck begins his study of preaching in Israel with a description of the schema of history which could be called deuteronomistic, as set out simply in 2 Kings 17:7-20.[1] The scheme consists of four parts.

(A) The people sin.
(B) God patiently warns them through the prophets.
(C) They remain stiff-necked.
(D) God punishes them.

2 Kings 17 explains the destruction of the northern and southern kingdoms according to this scheme. Thus what Steck refers to as the deuteronomistic scheme of history corresponds to the final view of the Deuteronomistic history, i.e., with the view of the final editor of that history as explained by Cross.[2]

Steck sees the pattern altered in the additions at the beginning and the end of Dtn.[3] In Dtn 4:25-31 the pattern becomes the following.

---

[1]O. H. Steck, *Israel und das gewaltsame Geschick der Propheten*, Neukirchen-Vluyn: Neukirchener Verlag, 1967, pp. 66ff.

[2]F. M. Cross, *Canaanite Myth and Hebrew Epic*, Cambridge, Mass.: Harvard, 1973, pp. 274-289.

[3]Steck, pp. 139ff. The later scheme as found in Dtn is also found in the Testaments of the Twelve Patriarchs: sin-punishment-repentance-redemption (pp. 150ff). Steck asserts (pp. 151-152) that in the Testaments, the author sees his own time as that of sin and punishment, and looks to the future for repentance and restoration.

(A) The people sin.
D) God punishes them.
(E) The people repent.
(F1) The people return to the land and prosperity.

This pattern also appears in Dtn 28:45-68 and 30:1-10. In Dtn 30:1-10, in addition to F1, i.e., the restoration of the people, we find F2, i.e., the punishment of the enemies of the people.[4]

As Steck traces the scheme he has isolated through various pieces of literature, he stresses the homiletic use of it. In order to move the people to repentance, through which they must pass in order to reach the restoration, the preacher characterizes the present as a time of punishment.

Steck includes 2B in his body of literature with connections to the deuteronomistic scheme of history. In 2B, the scheme exists without the employment of the theme of the prophetic missions to Israel, as is also true of Dtn. The chart on the following page shows how Steck believes the author of 2B to have used the scheme.[5] It is not surprising for us to realize that he has found the pattern in the two major speeches of Baruch at the end of sections III (31:1-32:7) and IV (44:1-46:7). The scheme is one which has exhortation as its purpose and in these two speeches we have Baruch exhorting the people. The same holds true for the occurrence of the scheme in section VII, the epistle, where Steck also finds it. The basic thrust of the exhortation of Baruch to the people is that they have sinned and are therefore being punished, and that if they repent by a renewed dedication to the Law, they will reach their reward. Thus Steck is quite correct in remarking that Baruch's exhortation is based as much upon a look to the future as to the past.

I disagree with Steck when he sees 2B 4:2-6 (the heavenly city) as an instance of F1, the reward of the obedient. In its present location, the reference to the heavenly city serves to denigrate the earthly one, as we explained in chapter four. Its presence in heaven is not meant as a punishment as such. On the other hand, it does connect with chapter 51, where the description of heaven itself (this time without explicit mention of the city) is used as element F1, in my opinion.

---

[4]Steck sees a development in his element F2 (punishment of the enemies) in that from the time of the Hasideans onward, the ones who will be punished in the future include not only non-Israelite enemeies, but also sinful Israelites.

[5]Steck, pp. 181-182.

	1:1–4:6	31:1–32:7	44:1–46:7	77:1–17	EPISTLE
A	1:2ff		44:6	77:4a, 10	78:5-6 79:2
D	1:4ff	31:4; 32:2ff	44:5ff	77:4b, (8-10)	78:5ff 84:4ff 79:1-3 80
E		31:3 32:1	44:3 (7a); 45:1 44:3, 7a, 14; 46:5, 6a	77:2 77:6a, 16	78:6; 83:8 84:6ff 85:4, 7ff
F1	4:2-6	32:4, 6b	44:7b, 8b, 12a, 13 44:15a; 46:6a	77:6-7	78:7; 38:4ff 84:6 85:8ff
F2		31:5	44:12b, 15b; 46:6b		Chs 82ff 85:8ff

Steck points out that the author uses the scheme at the beginning and the end of the major portion of the book (sections I-VI, excluding the epistle). If we are right in not considering 2B 4:2-6 as functioning as F1 of the scheme, then in chapter 1 we have only elements A and D. We are missing elements E and F of the scheme as it is represented in the two speeches and in the epistle. I suggest that the author has quite consciously left the scheme open-ended at this point, and thereby has created a certain tension. 1:5 probably anticipates the resolution of this tension.

> And my people shall be chastened, and the time shall come
> when they will seek for the prosperity of their times.

Whatever this somewhat strange expression means, it would appear to refer to some sort of change of heart on the part of the people. In any case, chapter 1 sets up a tension between God and his people. Baruch's exhortation in the book, based upon God's instruction of him, stresses the scheme of history isolated by Steck. However, it is only in chapter 77 that the change of heart of the people is absolutely clear. There they assent to Baruch explicitly. This corresponds to element E, repentance. F1 and F2 (reward of the good and punishment of the wicked) are the subject of much of the book as the author describes the future world, but these elements are especially represented by chapters 49-51.

Steck has suggested as a *Sitz im Leben* for the use of the deuteronomistic scheme of history the preaching which would accompany the renewal of the covenant.[6] As Baltzer notes in his study of the covenant formulary, once the people have sinned, the covenant must be renewed.[7] The preacher explains the present distress as a punishment for sin, and the people must respond in some way to indicate their acceptance of that interpretation and their return to the Law. Therefore the covenant renewal and the preaching described by Steck converge.

DEUTERONOMY AND SECOND BARUCH

A very common form in Deuteronomy is the conditional sentence in which the protasis deals with obedience to God's Law, and the apodosis

---

[6]Steck, pp. 133ff and 215ff. On p. 134 he suggests that covenant renewal was a regular celebration after the Exile, and was perhaps associated with the feast of Weeks.

[7]K. Baltzer, *The Covenant Formulary*, Philadelphia: Fortress, 1971, pp. 51ff.

with the reward for obedience to that Law. This form occurs some 14 times in the book. The chart which follows condenses these sentences. They differ from the numerous other conditional sentences in Dtn in that both the protases and the apodoses are very general, giving the appearance of general principles rather than specific laws.

4:25	IF you make a graven image, THEN you will perish from the land.
4:29	IF you search for God with your heart and soul, THEN you will find him, and he will remember the covenant.
11:13	IF you obey the commands, and love God with your heart and soul, THEN there will be rain and grass.
11:22	IF you are careful to do the commands, and to love him, THEN he will drive out the nations before you.
*11:27	IF you obey the commands, THEN the blessing will come.
11:28	IF you do not obey, THEN the curses will come.
13:18	IF you obey the commands, THEN he will have mercy on you and multiply you.
15:5	IF you obey and do the commands, THEN he will bless you in the land.
*28:1	IF you obey, THEN you will be blessed above all nations, there will be fertility and the land will be yours.
28:15	If you do not obey, THEN curses will fall on the city and the land.
28:58	IF you are not careful to perform the book of the law, THEN there will be plagues and exile.
30:10	IF you obey with your heart and soul, THEN you will be prosperous and there will be fruit from the ground, etc.
*30:16	IF you obey, THEN you will live and multiply and he will bless you in the land.
30:17	IF you do not obey, you will perish from the land.

In Dtn the form of the conditional sentence is closely tied to the blessings and curses section of the covenant formulary. In three instances two
conditional sentences are paired, the first telling what will happen when
the people obey the Law, and the second what will happen if they do not
do so (see starred sentences). (11:27-28; 28:1, 15; 30:16-17) In two cases,
chapters 11 and 28, it is explicitly said that the consequences in question
fall into the categories of blessings and curses. In the third case, chapter
30, the context makes clear that the consequences are conceived of in the
same terms (cf. 30:19). Blessings and curses are of course part of the
covenant formulary as discussed by Baltzer.

The conditional form also occurs outside of these strictly parallel
instances. In every case but one, it is the result of positive action which is
stipulated. (The exception is Dtn 4:25.) This shows that the form, originally associated by Dtn with a covenant ceremony, is used in a somewhat
wider context in the book as a whole, and this use corresponds to the
generally hortatory tone of Dtn.[8] The book tries to spur the people to
obedience to the Law by setting before them the positive results of such a
course of action.

Dtn is in the form of a long speech by Moses to the people of Israel
shortly before they enter the promised land to possess it.[9] Most of the
apodoses of the conditional form describe something to do with the land.
Obedience to the Law brings about possession of the land (11:22), blessings
in the land (15:5) which can be further specified as rain (11:13) and grass,
as fertility (30:10; 28:1ff), and life and multiplication in the land (30:16).
The negative results of disobedience involve perishing "from the land"
(4:25; 30:17) and curses falling upon city, field, etc. (28:15ff).[10] 28:58ff
makes clear that punishment also involves exile, a topic which is treated
in 4:25-31 at greater length, again in the context of an exhortation involving the use of the conditional form. The frequency of the conditional form
in Dtn shows that much of the exhortation of the book is based upon
displaying to the people the consequences of their obedience or disobedience to the Law.

---

[8]G. von Rad, *Deuteronomy, A Commentary*, London: S.C.M., 1966, p.
19.

[9]Von Rad, p. 12.

[10]I am aware that in form these clauses are not blessings and curses.
In content and function, they are related.

The conditional form as described above for Dtn is also found often in 2B. It occurs 14 times in all:

| 32:1 | But as for you, if you prepare your hearts, so as to sow in them fruits of the law, it shall protect you in that time in which the Mighty One is to shake the whole creation. |

| 44:7 | For if you endure and persevere in his fear, and do not forget his law, the times shall change over you for good, and you shall see the consolation of Zion. |

| 46:5 | But only prepare your hearts that you may obey the law, and be subject to those who in fear are wise and understanding; and prepare your souls that you may not depart from them. |

| 46:6 | For if you do these things, good tidings shall come to you. |

| *75:7 | But if, indeed, we who exist know wherefore we have come and submit ourselves to Him who brought us out of Egypt, we shall come again and remember those things which have passed, and shall rejoice regarding that which has been. |

| *75:8 | But if now we know not wherefore we have come, and recognize not the principate of Him who brought us up out of Egypt, we shall come again and seek after those things which have been now, and be grieved with pain because of those things which have befallen. |

| 77:6 | If, therefore, you direct your ways aright, you also shall not depart as your brethren departed, but they shall come to you. |

| *77:16 | If therefore you have respect to the law, and are intent upon wisdom, a lamp will not be wanting, and a shepherd will not fail, and a fountain will not dry up. |

| 78:6 | Therefore, if you consider that you have now suffered those things for your good, that you may not finally be condemned and tormented, then you will receive eternal hope. If above all you destroy from your heart vain error, on account of which you departed hence. |

78:7   For if you so do these things, He will continu-
              ally remember you, He who always promised on
              our behalf to those who were more excellent
              than we, that He will never forget or forsake
              us, but with much mercy will gather together
              again those who were dispersed.

*84:2   If you transgress the law you shall be dispersed,
              but if you keep it you shall be kept.

*84:6   If you obey those things which have been said to
              you, you will receive from the Mighty One
              whatever has been laid up and reserved for you.

85:4   If therefore we direct and dispose our hearts,
              we shall receive everything that we lost, and
              much better things than we lost by many times.

We have made the point in chapter two of this thesis that the purpose
of 2B is primarily that of exhortation to obedience to the Law. Its purpose
therefore is generally the same as that of Dtn. The hortatory purpose
expressed itself graphically in 2B by the general movement of the book
from the prayers of Baruch, through God's instructions to him, to Baruch's
instruction and exhortation of the people. The real point of the book is to
be found in the exhortation of the people. It is to be expected, then, that
we find the conditional form in 2B confined primarily to the speeches of
Baruch to the people, and to the letter to the Dispersion which comprises
section VII of the book. As in Dtn, 2B uses this conditional form to exhort
the people to obedience by setting before them the consequences of
obedience. As in Dtn, there is a greater emphasis on blessings than curses.

In two instances in 2B, we find two conditional sentences placed in
parallel (starred in the preceding list), the first denoting the result of
obedience to the Law, and the second the result of disobedience (75:7-8
and 84:2-6). In chapter 84, the context of a covenant is clear, as we will
explain below. The very language as well as the form of 75:7-8 suggests a
covenantal context. As in Dtn the conditional form is also used outside of
these two instances in a somewhat wider context, i.e., that of general
exhortation to obedience to the Law.

We must pay special attention to the similarities and differences
between Dtn's use of this form and 2B's. Both exhort to obedience to the
Law. This is explicit in 2B 32:1; 44:7; 46:5; 77:16; 84:2, 6. It is in looking
at the results of obedience of the Law that we begin to see the sharp
difference between Dtn and 2B. Whereas Dtn expects that possession of
the land and prosperity in it are the rewards of obedience, 2B has a more

eschatological view. This is especially clear in 32:1, where obedience to the Law will protect one in the final tribulations, and in 78:6 where it is an "eternal hope" which is promised. This is further supported by the promise in 85:4 that the people would receive much more than they had lost. This promise is located in a chapter which shows that those things which had been lost were nothing compared to what will come in the new world.

Promises about return to the land may seem to be behind the apodoses in 77:6 and 78:7. In fact, all that these verses promise is the eventual reunion of Israel. Read in the light of chapters 49-51, this reunion takes place in the new world.

The other promises expressed in the apodoses of the conditional sentences in 2B are more vague, and therefore to understand their import one must read them in the context of the book as a whole, particularly as analyzed in the previous two chapters of this thesis. As has been previously observed, the promise of the "consolation of Zion" in 44:7 does not refer to a rebuilding of the earthly sanctuary, but rather of the entrance of the chosen people into the presence of God. In 46:6, the "good tidings" are said to have been discussed before by Baruch. The obvious referent for these "tidings" is the immediately preceding speech in which Baruch described at some length the two worlds and contrasted them. Again, the promise of 46:6 is an eschatological one, and the reward is entrance into the other world into which Baruch is now going. (Chapter 43)

84:2 is a recollection of the establishment of the Mosaic Covenant, specifically as it is presented in Dtn 4 and 30. This is clear from the invocation of heaven and earth as witnesses to the covenant. Accordingly, violation of the covenant is said to bring dispersion, as in Dtn 4. Since this is the present position of the people for the author, this form of the conditional sentence serves him well, for it explains once again the reason for the present dispersion. In 84:6, Baruch is re-establishing the covenant. In this re-establishment, the promise is shifted to an eschatological context. The people are not said to receive the land back, as in Dtn, but are to obtain "whatever has been laid up and reserved" for them. The word "reserved" is from the root *ntr*, which has eschatological overtones for 2B. What has been laid up for the people is the other world, as can be seen in chapter 44 and chapters 49-51.

We must conclude that 2B has altered the point of view of Dtn. The structure of the exhortation of 2B is the same as that of Dtn. Both use the promise of future blessing to give the people an incentive to obey the Law. In Dtn the blessings center upon the land. In 2B, the author has chosen to deal with the loss of Zion and the exile of the people from the land by relativizing the situation. He does this by showing that the real fulfilment of the promises can only take place in God's eternal presence in heaven. Accordingly, the apodoses of his conditional sentences are either somewhat vague and therefore tend to be read in the context of the entire book or refer quite plainly to an eschatological reward in which no mention is made of the promised land.

In the apodosis of 2B 77:16, the author has adapted the conditional form to his concern for continued leadership in the community.[11] Thus if the people cleave to the Law, leaders will be supplied to them. This concern has also affected the protasis of 46:5.

In 75:7-8, the apodoses are adapted to Baruch's immediate concern to counter an attitude of wrongful mourning among his contemporaries. True submission to God will result in joy over what has happened and not sorrow. Sorrow becomes a sign that one has not truly submitted oneself to God.

We have observed that the author of 2B moves the exhortation of Dtn into an eschatological context. He also introduces two other of his specific concerns into the form of the conditional sentence, namely his interest in the continuation of leadership within the congregation, and his desire to correct an attitude of mourning over the loss of Zion.

The use of the generalized conditional sentence in the parenetic context is a phenomenon which is found also in Lev 26, thus in a priestly context.[12] I have analyzed this form in 2B with reference to Dtn because of other connections between the two books which make it seem likely that the author of 2B patterned Baruch upon Moses as presented in Dtn.

Pastoral Exhortation in Dtn and 2B

2B picks up a tendency of Dtn which von Rad explicates as an attempt "to move from specifically legal formulations towards pastoral exhortation and encouragement."[13] Dtn lays considerable emphasis upon the disposition of one's heart and soul.[14] This is found primarily outside of the conditional statement, but is found within it in 4:29, 11:13, and 30:10. In 2B, there is a frequent exhortation to prepare one's heart or one's soul.

---

[11]For this concern, see Sayler, *Promises*, pp. 74-85.
[12]I am indebted to Professor F. M. Cross for pointing this out to me.
[13]Von Rad, pp. 19-20.
[14]Gutbrod, article on *nomos* in *TDNT*, Volume IV, p. 1041.

This occurs both within the conditional form[15] and outside it.[16] In its occurrences outside of the form it makes clear that this activity of preparing one's heart is done with the future eschatological reward in mind. The following citations demonstrate the point.

> Make ready your soul for that which is reserved for you, and prepare your souls for the reward which is laid up for you. (52:7)

> Let none of these things (present) ascend into your hearts, but above all let us be expectant, because that which is promised to us shall come. (83:4)

> Do you therefore prepare your hearts for that which before you believed, lest you come to be in bondage in both worlds . . . (83:8)

> Let us prepare our soul that we may possess and not be taken possession of, and that we may hope and not be put to shame, and that we may rest with our fathers, and not be tormented with our enemies. (85:9)

> And again prepare your souls, so that when you sail and ascend from the ship you may have rest and not be condemned when you depart. (85:11)

Remembrance in Dtn and 2B

The word "remember," sometimes paired with the word "forget," is extremely frequent in Dtn. Although the word plays an important role in various parts of the Old Testament, this is especially true of Dtn. Michel says: "Dt. especially develops a theology of remembering (Dt. 5:15; 7:18; 8:2, 18; 9:7; 15:15; 16:3, 12; 24:18, 20, 22; 32:7). The severe visitation in Egypt should especially be remembered by Israel . . . and should lead them to new obedience and trust, and to the avoidance of disobedience and arrogance."[17] Dtn encourages Israel to remember that it had been a slave in Egypt, and that God had rescued it from there. This is equivalent to remembering the good that God had done for them in the past. Further,

---

[15] 2B 32:1; 46:5; 78:6; 85:4.

[16] 2B 52:7; 83:4; 83:8; 85:9; 85:11.

[17] O. Michel, article on *mimnesko* in *TDNT*, Volume IV, pp. 675-683.

they are not to forget the covenant (4:23) or the Lord himself (6:12; 8:18) or his commands (8:11, 14). Finally, in 30:1, the people are told to remember the blessing and the curse associated with the covenant, when they finally end up in exile.

In 2B the word "remember" (both the roots *dkr* and *ʿhd* are used) occurs 26 times and the word "forget" (*tʿʾ*) 14 times. Thus the pair of verbs is at least as prominent in 2B as in Dtn. All of the major objects of the verbs as found in Dtn are also present in 2B. The people are to remember the good the Lord has done for them (48:29; three times in 77:11; 78:3). They are to remember the covenant (84:2) and God's Law (48:38; 84:7; 84:8; 44:7). They should also remember the good or evil consequences of their actions, equivalent to the blessings and curses of Dtn (50:1; 48:7; 83:5; 82:8).

2B extends his use of this language beyond that of Dtn. Whereas God's remembrance of the people is important in Dtn 5:33, in 2B 48:7 God's remembrance extends to the "beginning" and the "end" of all that he has made. God's control over all creation and the inevitability of his plan are stressed here. We have moved into an apocalyptic worldview. This is also true in 23:3, where God "remembers" the people who are yet to come into the world, and paces his plans accordingly. In 78:6 we are closer to Dtn in that the promise is that God will not forget Israel. However, in 25:4 a sign of the endtime is that people say that God no longer remembers the *earth*. This is a challenge to God's very sovereignty over the earth and its happenings.

There are two uses of the words "remember" and "forget" which are peculiar to 2B. The first is the command to remember Zion (31:4; also 44:5, although the actual word "remember" is not used). I claimed in the last chapter that the author picks up a slogan of his opponents here and adapts it to his own purposes. The second is that forgetfulness of the present time with all of its evils is one of the traits of the other world. (43:2; 19:7; 44:9) This fits in with the author's purposes in dealing with a mournful attitude towards what had happened to Zion. He claims that in the other world, the righteous will not even remember what happened.

As we saw above, the author adapts the form of the conditional sentence which he found in Dtn and adapted it to his own purposes, leaving the form itself intact. We now see that he does the same with Dtn's language of remembering and forgetting. He shares all of Dtn's usages of these terms, but goes beyond them in ways which pertain directly to his own concerns.

Baruch Paralleled to Moses

There is evidence that the author intended to parallel Baruch and his activity with Moses and his activity, specifically as seen in Dtn. This is clearest in chapter 84 where Baruch's work in exhorting the people to the covenant and writing the epistle is compared with Moses' work in establishing the covenant. As Moses established the covenant, Baruch re-establishes it. In the description of the Mosaic covenant, Moses calls upon heaven and earth as witnesses. This goes back to Dtn 4 and 30. The same passages from Dtn are used in 2B 19 to stress the personal responsibility of each person in obeying or not.

All of Dtn is a testament.[18] The book is presented as Moses' final words to the people before he passes his authority on to Joshua and dies. Although this cannot be said about 2B without qualification, nonetheless the book does contain what all admit to be a testament in chapter 44. The setting of the book is the destruction of Jerusalem and the revelations of God to Baruch and of Baruch to the people following upon that catastrophe. That part of the revelation to Baruch is that he is about to leave this life (chapter 43) makes his instructions to the people a testament. This is formally true of chapter 44, but it can fairly be said that this situation colors all of Baruch's words to Israel.[19]

The parallel between Baruch and Moses is further sharpened in chapter 76. As in Dtn 34, Moses is told to ascend the mountain to look at the land which he will not enter and which he now leaves behind through death, so also Baruch is in chapter 76 told to ascend a mountain in order to view all which he is about to leave behind. Our author bends this image to his own purposes. Whereas Moses looks at the promised land which is the object of God's promises, Baruch is to contemplate the earth as a region about to pass away, and one which he will soon forget. (chapter 43) The author thus graphically portrays the difference between his view and that of Dtn as we explicated above. Dtn sees the land as the reward for obedience, but 2B feels that all, including the land, must pass away. It cannot be the locus for the fulfilment of the promises. Baruch becomes a paradigm for all of the righteous who in chapters 49-51 make the same journey he makes here. They also leave this corruptible world and forget all of its troubles. (44:9)

There is of course the more general parallel between Moses and

---

18Von Rad, p. 22.
19Sayler, *Promises*, pp. 95-98.

Baruch, not necessarily connected to the book of Dtn, in that both are intermediaries between God and Israel. As Moses left the people and ascended the mountain to receive God's instruction, so also Baruch leaves the people and ascends Mount Zion in order to receive God's instruction. Both intermediaries then carry the instruction back to the people.

Just as Moses addresses the people, "Hear, O Israel," in Dtn 5:1 and 9:1, so Baruch addresses them in the same way in 2B 31:3. In chapter 77, when Baruch addresses the people he uses a very similar phrase, "Hear, ye children of Israel." Just as Moses summons "all Israel" to hear his words in Dtn 1:1 and again in 29:2, so also Baruch in chapter 77 summons the people, "from the greatest to the least."

In Dtn Moses is depicted as a teacher (4:1, 14; 5:31; 6:1; 31:22). As he dies, he is concerned that the Law which he has taught the people will be taught by them to their children (Dtn 11:19; 4:10). Similarly, Baruch is pictured as a teacher of the people, and as one who is concerned that after his death there will be persons (now a special class) who will continue to teach the people. (Chapters 44-45 and 84:9)

Chapter 45 of 2B, just mentioned, says that the activity of the teachers in teaching the Law is life-giving (45:1-2). This is because God's Law is life (38:2). This implies that the activity of the teachers is in some degree analogous to that of Moses when he founded the covenant, as it is described in Dtn 30:19, and drawn upon in 2B 19. In 2B 46:3, faced with the death of Baruch, the people ask,

> For where again shall we seek the Law, or who will distinguish for us between life and death?

The Law as life is a reoccurring theme in Dtn (4:1; 5:33; 30:16; 30:10; 32:47; 6:2). In Dtn, Moses' teaching takes place in order that the people may have life:

> And now, O Israel, give heed to the statutes and the ordinances which I teach you, and do them; that you may live and go in and take possession of the land . . . which the Lord, the God of your fathers gives you. (Dtn 4:1)

Wisdom and Understanding

In Dtn 4:6, the Law is said to be the wisdom and understanding of Israel, by possession of which they are wise and understanding.[20] In Dtn 32:38, the sinful people are a people with no understanding. They are unwise because they do not "discern their latter end."

"Wisdom and understanding" (ḥkm and śkl) is an important collocation of terms in 2B. "Wisdom" occurs 21 times, 11 times in connection with "understanding." In 28:1 it is the wise who can understand the imminence of the endtime. In 44:14 and 51:3 and 5, it is the wise and understanding who obtain the future life, which, of course, could be considered their "latter end." As in Dtn, wisdom and understanding are said in 2B to be associated with the Law (44:14; 51:3, 4, 7; chapter 38). In 2B, however, the "latter end" has become eschatological, and in chapters 49-51 is placed by the author into his specific eschatology.

Smaller Points of Contact

There are smaller points of contact between the two books. In Dtn 9:25ff there is a recollection of Moses' intercession for Israel on Sinai. In the previous chapter we showed how this incident was put into a form we called intercessory bargaining. Here that form has not been preserved. Nonetheless, the picture of Baruch in 2B 1-9 is drawn from the figure of the intercessor, and especially of Moses. That such a characterization of Moses is recalled in Dtn 9:25ff strenthens our case on this point.

The frequency with which the "elders" are mentioned in 2B may go back to their presence in Dtn (5:23; 27:1; 29:10; 31:28).

That God shows no partiality is a theme which occurs more than once in 2B (13:8; 44:4). It also occurs in Dtn 10:17.

In Dtn the presence of the people in the land and the presence of God among them, having a place called by his name in Zion, causes fertility, which is destroyed by the sin of the people (11:17). In 2B 10, Baruch informs the earth that it is no longer to be fertile because God is no longer present in the cult.

---

[20]For the connection between Dtn and wisdom circles, see M. Weinfeld, *Deuteronomy and the Deuteronomic School*, Oxford: Clarendon, 1972, especially pp. 244ff.

Baruch's concern with God's name in section I corresponds to the "name" theology of Dtn.[21] This "name" theology is strong throughout Dtr (the Deuteronomistic work).

In 2B 84 there is an emphasis upon the writing of the letter as a witness. This same emphasis upon the actual writing of the book of Dtn is seen in Dtn 28:61; 17:18ff; 30:10; 31:11. Also, Moses sees his song in chapter 31 as a witness against the people (31:21).[22]

In 2B there is, in spite of the numerous revelations in the book, a guarding of God's ultimate mysteries. This becomes evident when one notices that although God's incomprehensibility is a matter of some frustration for Baruch in chapter 14, this trait of God is nonetheless preserved when Baruch finds himself consoled and reconciled with God's plan in chapter 75. This sort of idea is present in Dtn 29:29.

> The secret things belong to the Lord our God, but the things that are revealed belong to us and to our children forever, that we may do all the words of this law.

Similarly, unlike seers such as Enoch, and Abraham in the Apocalypse of Abraham, Baruch does not need to go to heaven to receive the revelations he does here, nor do the people need to go there to have Baruch transmit to them such revelations. As Dtn says,

> It is not in heaven, that you should say, 'Who will go up for us to heaven, and bring it to us, that we may hear it and do it?' (Dtn 30:12)

SUMMARY

The comparison of Dtn and 2B in the preceding pages has shown that there is a certain community of forms, language, and setting between the two books. I attribute this to the author's desire to present Baruch as renewing the work of Moses. In so doing, he has put the Law squarely in the center of the life of the people. This effort of his is given power and legitimacy by his use of Dtn. At the same time, he has put all of this endeavor into a very different context than that of Dtn. Rather than seeing all in the context of possession of the land, he actually uses the

---

[21] R. Abba, article on "Name" in *IDB*, Volume III, p. 503; Bietenhard, article on *onoma* in *TDNT*, Volume V, pp. 256-257.

[22] Baltzer, pp. 16-17.

parallelism he develops between Moses and Baruch to change the expectations of the people from possession of the land to entrance into the new
world.

The writers of Dtn had already painted the activity of Moses in the
colors of the covenant formulary and of the kind of preaching described
by Steck. Our author used these elements, expanded by means of his own
knowledge of the patterns in question, and crafted the structure of his
work accordingly. The result is a strong exhortation, based on traditional
covenant material, but in the context of the author's peculiar eschatology,
which is an eschatology in transition.

6

Conclusions and Prospectus
of Future Study

The purpose of this chapter is to recapitulate the major points of the previous chapters, and then to provide a prospectus for further study by proposing some tentative suggestions about the historical situation in which the author of 2B found himself and about his reaction to it.

RECAPITULATION

Chapter two of this dissertation provided a tool for the analysis of the other chapters by analyzing the literary structure of 2B. Without such an analysis, judgments about what ideas are central to the author and which ones are not are hard to make.

Chapter three investigated the author's concept of the two worlds. We found that he took up a notion current in his time and developed it by emphasizing the ontological differences between the two worlds. He describes the present world as essentially limited and transitory. He does this both by appeal to common experience (chapters 19 and 21 especially) and by use of the creation image (chapter 21). The essence of this world has been the same since the creation. The other world is equivalent to heaven but retains some language from the eschatology in the tradition of Isaiah.

In chapter four we showed that the absence of the Temple and Zion was the central concern of our author. He responded to this problem by placing the Temple firmly in this corruptible world, thus relativizing its importance. The passing of the world, which is inevitable, necessitates the passing away of Zion as well (chapter 20). This view of Zion contradicts a Temple ideology which cannot conceive of Israel, the Law, humanity, the world, etc. without the existence of the Temple and Zion. The use by the author of the intercession dialogue in section I illustrates particularly clearly the rejection of such a Temple ideology. This is confirmed by the reaction of God to Baruch's lament in chapters 10-12.

2B exhorts its readers to obedience to the Law. It does so by having Baruch exhort his listeners to obedience. In chapter five I demonstrated the close connection of the thought of the author to the forms and ideas evident in the preaching of the covenant especially as contained in Deuteronomy. Our author has made Baruch look and sound much like Moses in Dtn. The author adapts the covenant idea to his view of the two worlds by substituting entrance into the other world for possession of the land as a reward for Israel's fidelity to the covenant. Entrance into the other world, and presence before God's throne are now seen as the blessing which flows from faithful adherence to the Law. The Law thus becomes the protector of the righteous when this world passes away (chapter 32).

PROSPECTUS FOR FURTHER STUDY:
HISTORICAL SITUATION OF 2B

The following pages contain a possible, and somewhat speculative, reconstruction of the historical situation in which 2B was composed. This reconstruction is based upon the analysis of 2B carried through in this thesis, but is of a more speculative nature than the conclusions found in the analysis itself. Further work, which would make more extensive use of contemporary documents and the most recent results of research on rabbinic literature,[1] could be based on the insights presented below.

It cannot be overlooked that it was in the defense of the Temple that the rebels against Rome put forth their greatest efforts. It is unlikely that that devotion to the Temple simply died out once it was destroyed. In fact, we know that some elements of resistance persisted throughout the next sixty to seventy years. In 132 C.E. war broke out again under Bar Kokba. In his recent book on the Bar Kokba uprising, P. Schäfer finds no evidence either of a literary or a numismatic nature to support the claim that Bar Kokba intended to rebuild Jerusalem and the Temple.[2] Nonetheless, it would be strange indeed if there were no elements left in Palestine after 70 C.E. who cherished a hope of a rebuilt Jerusalem. The point of the above remarks is that even after Jersualem was destroyed in 70 C.E.,

---

[1]See especially the work of Jacob Neusner and his students.

[2]Peter Schäfer, *Der Bar Kokhba-Aufstand*, Tübingen: Mohr, 1981, pp. 99-101.

it is probable that there were Jews in Palestine who looked forward to a rebuilding of the Temple in the near future. If 2B was written early in the second century C.E., that would place it as the beginning of the resistance described by Mantel.[3]

The author of 2B may have wanted to discourage this resistance movement by showing that it did not coincide with God's plans. To absolutize the Temple and the land is to ignore the very nature of the world as it can be perceived by experience (sapiental reasoning—chapter 21) and revelation (chapters 2-5, 20, 32, 49-51, etc.). One should rather put one's energies into obedience to the Law so that one can enter into the new world.

The way that 2B treats the enemies (i.e., the destroyers of Jerusalem) also supports this impression. As has been demonstrated in the previous chapters, it is never stated that the enemies are to be punished specifically for the destruction of Jerusalem. Rather, enemies and Jews alike are all to be judged and punished according to the same standard—the Law. Even where the feeling against the enemies seems most intense (chapters 82-83), the feeling is blunted and corrected by an individually conceived judgment process. The author in several places explicitly states that one should not worry about the judgment of the enemies, but instead should think of one's own judgment. This kind of approach, if followed through, would take the wind out of the sails of any movement seeking to overthrow the Romans and rebuild Zion.

This forms an interesting contrast to the Apocalypse of Abraham. If Mueller is correct, this document sees the Temple as absolutely central to Judaism. Because the Temple service was defiled, God allowed it to be destroyed.[4] The Apocalypse looks for a restoration of the Temple through the militant action of the faithful Jews. If it is correct to date this document at about the same period as 2B, and in Palestine, then we would perhaps be in direct contact with one of the points of view which the author of 2B wished to correct. As the Apocalypse of Abraham looks for the overthrow of the enemies and the rebuilding of the Temple, 2B takes attention away from the enemies and relativizes the importance of the Temple.

The same tendency of the author can also be perceived in his use of the word "hope" (sbr ʾ). In his use of this word we can trace his reorientation

---

[3]H. Mantel, "The Causes of the Bar Kokba Revolt," *JQR* 58 (1968), p. 239.

[4]R. Mueller, "The Apocalypse of Abraham and the Destruction of the Second Jewish Temple." SBLASP, Chico: Scholars, 1982, pp. 341-349.

of the hope of the people to the other world. In 70:5, the angel Ramiel says that in the final black waters,

> And the wise shall be silent, and the foolish shall speak, neither shall the thought of men be then confirmed, nor the counsel of the mighty, nor shall the hope of those who hope be confirmed.

The same period is described by God in 25:4 in the following manner:

> And it will come to pass when they say in their thoughts by reason of their great tribulation: "The Mighty One does no longer remember the earth"—yes, it will come to pass when they abandon hope, that the time will then awake.

It is possible that in these passages the author is speaking of the hope of those who hoped that God would restore the Temple and who despaired when he did not. On the other hand, in chapter 44, the important testamentary speech of Baruch, Baruch says,

> Because whatever is now is nothing, but that which shall be is very great. For everything that is corruptible shall pass away, and everything that dies shall depart, and all the present time shall be forgotten, nor shall there be any remembrance of the present time which is defiled by evils. For that which runs now unto vanity, and that which prospers shall quickly fall and be humiliated. For that which is to be shall be the object of desire, and for that which comes afterwards shall we hope. For it is a time which passes not away, and the hour comes which abides forever.

These words fall in the section of the testament which compares the two worlds in detail. The obvious alternative to hope in the other world is hope in this world. This the author discourages.

In 59:10, Moses is shown "the place of faith, and the region of hope." We have already made the case that faith (or belief—hymnwt ɔ) refers to belief in the future world.[5] Here this is paralleled to hope. The author means that Moses learned of the future world and that true hope lies there and not in the present world.

The use of the word "hope" in 63:3 is particularly informative. We have

---

[5]See chapter five of this thesis.

suggested that the author is arguing against those that would resist Rome and rebuild Zion. In chapter 63, which occurs within the review of history, Hezekiah's time is the subject. At a time when Zion was in danger from the forces of Sennacherib, Hezekiah hoped not in military strength but in his works and righteousness. As a result, Zion was saved. This would contrast sharply with the military methods by which some of the author's contemporaries would choose to oust Rome.

The activity which is advocated by our author is obedience to the Law. It is understandable, then, when he claims that Hezekiah hopes in his works and righteousness. As 51:7 says, the Law is a hope to those who will be saved.

In 77:12, the people ask Baruch to write to the Dispersion an "epistle of doctrine and a scroll of hope." They are asking that he do for their fellows what he has done for them. He has given them hope by giving them the doctrine of the two worlds. Once they have accepted the new world as the goal, they may hope for their inclusion in it. In 78:6, Baruch tells the Dispersion that they will receive "eternal hope" if they admit that what they have suffered has been for their own good. Such a confession would be out of place on the lips of those who still expected that an overthrow of Rome was in the offing.

We know that Akiba supported Bar Kokba's war.[6] Saldarini goes further and says that it is simplistic to see the rabbis as a group as pacifistic.[7]

> Between A.D. 70 and 132 the Jews in Palestine recovered from their defeat and geared up for another revolt. If Mantel's reading of the evidence is correct, the Jews were a rebellious and troublesome people (from a Roman point of view) and spent a long time building up to their second revolt. During this period the rabbinic leaders consolidated their position as religious leaders and teachers of Judaism and engaged in some of their most productive adaptations of the Jewish law. To say that they were completely pacifist would be to cut them off from the main stream of Jewish emotional and political life.

---

[6]Mantel, pp. 289ff.

[7]A. Saldarini, "Apocalyptic and Rabbinic Literature," *CBQ* 37 (1975), p. 357.

He states further:[8]

> The account of Johanan ben Zakkai's escape from Jerusalem,
> the keystone of the pacifist interpretation of Johanan and
> other rabbinic leaders, especially after A.D. 70, occurs in
> four versions and a comparison of the four suggests that
> details about the siege and the conflict of zealots and
> Johanan were added later.

In fact, it is somewhat simplistic to speak of "the rabbis" at all in the
period between the two revolts, because there were undoubtedly many
groups within the movement which we might call "rabbinic" at that time.
It is likely that there were both quietist and militant groups during the
inter-war period. If that is so, and if our interpretation of 2B as a pacifist
work is accurate, then the Apocalypse of Abraham and 2B represent
different sides of the debate which must have taken place.

The relation of 2B to apocalyptic as a whole is one which requires
further study, as does the thorny issue of apocalyptic itself. We can make
one comment here, though. If apocalyptic was being used by some mili-
tants to stir the people to revolt, as the Apocalypse of Abraham seems to
suggest, then our author may have chosen the genre of apocalypse in order
to counter the influence of such works. One might say that he uses the
apocalypse in an anti-apocalyptic way, especially if Sayler and others are
right in seeing part of his purpose to contradict any imminent expectation
of the eschaton.[9] Even the hope that the author does offer is delayed.

There has been a great deal of discussion of the relation between 2B
and 4E. A detailed exposition of my own position must wait for a separate
study. Here I wish only to indicate briefly what this study may contribute
to the debate. I have already stated in my analysis of chapter 4 in chapter
four of this thesis, that whereas in 4E the new Zion is found upon earth in
episode 4 of the book, in 2B the heavenly city never descends. The scene
of the final reward of the righteous remains in heaven. When this is seen
in combination with the desire of the author to avoid stirring any passions
against the enemies of Zion, and with his wisdom-like meditations on the

---

[8]Saldarini, "Rabbinic," pp. 356-357. See also his articles: "The Uses of
Apocalyptic in the Mishna and Tosephta," *CBQ* 39, (1977), pp. 396-409;
"Johanan ben Zakkai's Escape from Jerusalem: Origin and Development of
a Rabbinic Story," *JSJ* 6 (1975), pp. 189-204.

[9]G. Sayler, *Have the Promises Failed?*, SBLDS 72, 1984, pp. 14-38, 98-
102.

nature of this world, one may see that our author is not political in the way that 4E is. He also does not see the concrete events of history as significant in the same way as does 4E.

The first three episodes of 4E picture Ezra arguing vigorously against the angel Uriel because the political situation is a contradiction of God's promises. Episode 4 sees the divinely built city on earth, and episode 5 is entirely given over to a vision and interpretation whose sole purpose is to predict the overthrow of the enemies, Rome in particular, specifically for destroying the chosen people. The division and antagonism between Jew and Gentile is constitutive for the outlook of 4E.[10]

Although Baruch does rage against the enemies in chapters 11 and 12, I have shown how God corrects this attitude of his. Furthermore, the vision and interpretation of chapters 36-40, in which the overthrow of the enemies is depicted, are not the main point of section IV, as the vision and interpretation are of episode 5 of 4E. The vision and interpretation of section VI of 2B do not concern the punishment of the enemies but demonstrate the personal responsibility of both Jews and Gentiles for their punishment. Even though I believe that 2B's main interest is in the Jewish community, the book blurs the distinction between that community and the Gentiles because his interest is in exhortation to obedience to the Law as a means to get to the future world rather than in righting the wrongs of political oppression done to the chosen people by their enemies on this earth.

The observations above may help to explain the difference in emphasis between 2B and 4E. Sayler has pointed to the similarity in the two books in that in each of them the seer is consoled. She sees this "narrative world" as the key to the structure of 2B, as Breech had considered it the key to the structure of 4E.[11] Most commentators have remarked, however, that Baruch is in much less need of consolation than is Ezra. In fact, the figure of Ezra dominates 4E in a way that Baruch does not dominate 2B. Ezra's story is *the* story of 4E. It has been observed that Ezra spends very little time exhorting the people. In 2B Baruch's own consolation and correction is only part of the story. His exhortation of the people is an equally important part. This exhortation involves not only consolation, but also disuasion from a mistaken desire for the re-establishment of a political entity for Israel and for the punishment of the enemies of Zion. The

---

[10] *Pace* A. Thompson, *Responsibility for Evil in the Theodicy of IV Ezra*, Missoula: Scholars, 1977, pp. 157ff.

[11] Sayler, *Promises*, pp. 123-134.

author wants to put the Law at the center of Judaism and to establish the teachers of that Law as the guides to the future life.

Much work needs to be done on the few documents which give us any information about what was happening within Judaism between 70 and 132 C.E. I am hopeful that this dissertation will prove to be another forward step in the process of achieving a more satisfactory understanding of that period.

Bibliography

Abba, Raymond, "Name," *IDB*, Volume 3, pp. 500-508.

Anderson, Bernhard W., "Creation," *IDB*, Volume 1, pp. 725-732.

Bachmann, Michael B., *Jerusalem und der Tempel: Die Geographisch-theologischen Elemente in der lukanischen Sicht des jüdischen Kultzentrums,* Berlin: Kohlhammer, 1980.

Baltzer, Klaus, *The Covenant Formulary in Old Testament, Jewish and Early Christian Writings,* Philadelphia: Fortress, 1971.

Barrett, C. K., *A Commentary on the Second Epistle to the Corinthians,* London: Black, 1973.

Betz, Hans Dieter, *Galatians,* Philadelphia: Fortress, 1979.

Bietenhard, Hans, *onoma, TDNT,* Volume 5, pp. 242-283.

Bogaert, Pierre, *Apocalypse de Baruch: Introduction, Traduction du Syriaque et Commentaire,* SC 144 and 145, Paris: Le Cerf, 1969.

Brandenburger, Egon, *Adam und Christus: Exegetische-religionsgeschichtliche Untersuchung zu Röm.5:12-21 (1.Kor.15),* WMANT 7, Neukirchen: Neukirchener Verlag, 1962.

_____, *Fleisch und Geist,* WMANT 29, Neukirchen: Neukirchener Verlag, 1968.

_____, *Die Verborgenheit Gottes im Weltgeschehen: Das literarische und theologische Problem des 4. Esrabuches,* ATANT 68, Zürich: Theologischer Verlag Zürich, 1981.

Breech, Earl, "These Fragments I have Shored against My Ruins: The Form and Function of 4th Ezra," *JBL* 92 (1973), pp. 267-274.

Bultmann, Rudolf, *The History of the Synoptic Tradition*, Oxford: Blackwell, 1972.

Ceriani, A. M., *Monumenta Sacra et Profana. Opera Collegii Doctorum Bibliothecae Ambrosianae*, Tom. V, fasc. I/II, 1868/71.

Charles, R. H., *The Apocalypse of Baruch*, London: Black, 1896.

_____, *The Apocrypha and Pseudepigrapha of the Old Testament*, Oxford: Clarendon, 1913.

Collins, Adela Yarbro, *The Apocalypse*, Wilmington: Michael Glazier, 1979.

Collins, John J., ed., *Apocalypse: The Morphology of a Genre, Semeia* 14 (1979), SBL.

_____, "Apocalyptic Eschatology as the Transcendence of Death," *CBQ* 36 (1974), pp. 21-43.

_____, "The Biblical Precedent for Natural Theology," *JAAR* 15 (1977), Supplement B, pp. 35-67.

_____, "Cosmos and Salvation: Jewish Wisdom and Apocalyptic in the Hellenistic Age," *History of Religions* 17 (1977), pp. 121-142.

_____, "The Date and Provenance of the Testament of Moses," in *Studies on the Testament of Moses*, G. W. E. Nickelsburg, Jr., ed., SBLSCS 4, Cambridge, Mass., SBL, 1973, pp. 15-32.

_____, "The Heavenly Representative the 'Son of Man' in the Similitudes of Enoch," in *Ideal Figures in Ancient Judaism: Profiles and Paradigms*, SBLSCS 12, John J. Collins and G. W. E. Nickelsburg, eds., Missoula: Scholars, 1980, pp. 111-133.

_____, "The Root of Immortality: Death in the Context of Jewish Wisdom," *HTR* 71 (1978), pp. 177-192.

Collins, M., "The Hidden Vessels in Samaritan Traditions," *JSJ* 3 (1972), pp. 92-116.

Conzelmann, Hans, *1 Corinthians*, Philadelphia: Fortress, 1975.

Cross, Frank Moore, *Canaanite Myth and Hebrew Epic: Essays in the History of the Religion of Israel*, Cambridge, Mass.: Harvard, 1973.

Davies, W. D., *The Territorial Dimension of Judaism*, Berkeley: University of California, 1982.

Dedering, S., ed., "Apocalypse of Baruch," *The Old Testament in Syriac*, Part 4, fasc. 3, Leiden: Brill, 1973.

Farmer, William R., *Maccabees, Zealots and Josephus*, New York: Columbia, 1956.

Fitzmyer, Joseph A., *The Gospel According to Luke (I-IX)*, AB 28, Garden City: Doubleday, 1981.

Fohrer, Georg, *Sion*, *TDNT*, Volume 7, pp. 292-319.

Gammie, John G., "Spatial and Ethical Dualism in Jewish Wisdom and Apocalyptic Literature," *JBL* 93 (1974), pp. 356-385.

Gärtner, Bertil, *The Temple and the Community in Qumran and the New Testament*, Cambridge: Cambridge University, 1965.

Gaston, Lloyd, *No Stone on Another: Studies in the Significance of the Fall of Jerusalem in the Synoptic Gospels*, Leiden: Brill, 1970.

Gutbrod, W., *nomos*, *TDNT*, Volume 4, pp. 1036-1091.

Hamerton-Kelly, R. G., "The Temple and the Origins of Jewish Apocalyptic," *VT* 20 (1970), pp. 1-15.

Hanson, Paul, "Apocalypse, Genre," *IDB Supplement*, pp. 27-28.

_____, "Apocalypticism," *IDB* Supplement, pp. 28-34.

Harnisch, Wolfgang, *Verhängnis und Verheissung der Geschichte: Untersuchungen zum Zeit- und Geschichtsverständnis im 4. Buch Esra und in der syr. Baruchapokalypse*, FRLANT 97, Göttingen: Vandenhoeck & Ruprecht, 1969.

Hartman, Lars, "The Function of Some So-called Apocalyptic Timetables," *NTS* 22 (1976), pp. 1-14.

Herodotus, *The Histories*, New York: Penguin, 1954, rev. 1972.

James, M. R., *The Biblical Antiquities of Philo*, Translations of Early Documents, Series I, Palestinian Jewish Texts (Pre-Rabbinic), London: SPCK, 1917.

Jenni, E., "Das Wort ʿolam im Alten Testament," *ZAW* 64 (1952), pp. 197-248.

Jeremias, Joachim, *paradeisos*, *TDNT* Volume 5, pp. 765-773.

Josephus, *The Jewish War*, LCL 203 and 210, Cambridge, Mass.: Harvard, Books I-III: 1976; Books IV-VII: 1979.

Klausner, Joseph, *The Messianic Idea in Israel: From Its Beginning to the Completion of the Mishnah*, New York: Macmillan, 1955.

Klijn, A. F. J., "The Sources and the Redaction of the Syriac Apocalypse of Baruch," *JSJ* 1 (1970), pp. 65-76.

Kmosko, M., ed., *Liber Apocalypseos Baruch filii Neriae . . . , Epistola Baruch filii Neriae*, Patrologia Syriaca 1:2, Paris: Firmin-Didot, 1907.

Kolenkow, Anitra, *An Introduction to II Bar. 53, 56-74: Structure and Substance*, unpublished dissertation, Harvard University, 1971.

Konigsveld, P. Sj. van, "An Arabic Manuscript of the Apocalypse of Baruch," *JSJ* 6 (1975), pp. 205-207.

Lohse, Eduard, *Sion, TDNT*, Volume 7, pp. 319-338.

MacRae, George, "The Heavenly Temple and Eschatology in the Letter to the Hebrews," *Semeia* 12, Missoula: Scholars, 1978, pp. 179-199.

Mantel, Hugo, "The Causes of the Bar Kokba Revolt," *JQR* 58 (1968), pp. 224-296.

Michel, O., *mimneskomai,TDNT*, Volume 4, pp. 675-683.

Mueller, James R., "The Apocalypse of Abraham and the Destruction of the Second Jewish Temple," SBLASP 1982, K. H. Richards, ed., pp. 341-349.

Murphy, Roland, "Psalms," *JBC*, Volume I, pp. 569-602.

Myers, Jacob M., *I & II Esdras*, AB 42, Garden City: Doubleday, 1974.

Neusner, Jacob, *The Development of a Legend: Studies on the Traditions concerning Yohanan ben Zakkai*, Leiden: Brill, 1970.

_____, *A Life of Yohanan ben Zakkai*, Leiden: Brill, 1962.

_____, "The Formation of Rabbinic Judaism: Yavneh (Jamnia) from A.D. 70 to 100," in *Aufstieg und Niedergang der Römischen Welt*, New York: De Gruyter, 1979, *Principat* (II) 19, pp. 3-42.

Nickelsburg, George W. E., *Jewish Literature Between the Bible and the Mishnah*, Philadelphia: Fortress, 1981.

von Nordheim, Eckhard, *Die Lehre des Alten: I: Das Testament als Literaturgattung im Judentum der Hellenistisch-Römischen Zeit*, Leiden: Brill, 1980.

Patai, Raphael, *Man and Temple in Ancient Jewish Myth and Ritual*, New York: Nelson, 1947.

Perrin, Norman, "Towards an Interpretation of the Gospel of Mark," in *Christology and a Modern Pilgrimage*, H. D. Betz, ed., Missoula: Scholars, 1974.

Plöger, Otto, *Theocracy and Eschatology*, Oxford: Blackwell, 1968.

von Rad, Gerhard, *Deuteronomy, a Commentary*, London: SCM, 1966.

Rössler, Dietrich, *Gesetz und Geschichte*, WMANT 3, Neukirchen: Neukirchener Verlag, 1960.

Rowland, Christopher, *The Open Heaven*, New York: Crossroad, 1982.

Safrai, S., "The Temple," in *Compendia Rerum Iudaicarum ad Novum Testamentum: Section One: The Jewish People in the First Century*, Volume 2, S. Safrai and M. Stern, eds., Assen: Van Gorcum, 1974, pp. 865-907.

Saldarini, Anthony, "Apocalyptic and Rabbinic Literature," *CBQ* 37 (1975) pp. 348-358.

_____, "Johanan ben Zakkai's Escape from Jerusalem: Origin and Development of a Rabbinic Story," *JSJ* 6 (1975), pp. 189-204.

_____, "The Uses of Apocalyptic in the Mishna and Tosephta," *CBQ* 39 (1977), pp. 396-409.

Sasse, H., *aion*, *TDNT*, Volume 1, pp. 197-209.

_____, *kosmeo*, *TDNT*, Volume 3, pp. 867-898.

Sayler, Gwendolyn, "2 Baruch: a Story of Grief and Consolation," SBLASP, Chico: Scholars, 1982, pp. 485-500.

_____, *Have the Promises Failed?*, SBLDS 72, 1984.

Schäfer, Peter, *Der Bar Kokhba-Aufstand: Studies zum zweiten judischen Krieg gegen Rom*, Texte und Studien zum Antiken Judentum 1, Tübingen: Mohr, 1981.

Smith, R. Payne, *A Compendious Syriac Dictionary*, J. Payne Smith, ed., Oxford: Clarendon, 1903.

Steck, Odil Hannes, *Israel und das gewaltsame Geschick der Propheten: Untersuchungen zur Überlieferung des Deuteronomistischen Geschichtsbildes im Alten Testament, Spätjudentum und Urchristentum*, Neukirchen: Neukirchener Verlag, 1967.

Stemberger, Günter, *Der Leib der Auferstehung: Studien zur Anthropologie und Eschatologie des palastinischen Judentums im neutestamentlischen Zeitalter (ca. 170 v. Cr. - 100 n. Chr.)*, An Bib 56, Rome: Biblical Institute, 1972.

Stone, Michael, *Features of the Eschatology of IV Ezra*, unpublished dissertation, Harvard University, 1965.

Strugnell, John, "Review of Books," *JBL* 89 (1970), pp. 484-485.

Thompson, Alden L., *Responsibility for Evil in the Theodicy of 4th Ezra*, SBLDS 29, Missoula: Scholars, 1977.

Vermes, Geza, *The Dead Sea Scrolls in English*, 2nd ed., Baltimore: Penguin, 1975.

Vielhauer, Paul, "Introduction" to chapter XVI ("Apocalyptic in Early Christianity") of Volume 2 of *New Testament Apocrypha*, E. Hennecke, ed. by W. Schneemelcher, Philadelphia: Westminster, 1964.

Violet, Bruno, *Die Apokalypsen des Esra und des Baruch in Deutscher Gestalt*, Leipzig: Hinrich, 1924.

Weinfeld, Moshe, *Deuteronomy and the Deuteronomic School*, Oxford: Clarendon, 1972.

Wenschkewitz, Hans, *Die Spiritualisierung der Kultusbegriffe*, Leipzig: Pfeiffer, 1932.

Winston, David, *The Wisdom of Solomon*, AB 43, Garden City: Doubleday, 1979.